The Somatic Therapy Workbook

The
Somatic
Therapy
Workbook

Stress-Relieving Exercises for Strengthening
the Mind-Body Connection and
Sparking Emotional and Physical Healing

LIVIA SHAPIRO

 ULYSSES PRESS

Published by:
Ulysses Press
P.O. Box 3440
Berkeley, CA 94703
www.ulyssespress.com

ISBN: 978-1-64604-095-7
Library of Congress Control Number: 2020936174

10 9 8 7 6 5 4 3 2

Acquisitions editor: Ashten Evans
Managing editor: Claire Chun
Editor: Pat Harris
Proofreader: Renee Rutledge
Front cover design: Rebecca Lown
Interior design and layout: what!design @ whatweb.com

IMPORTANT NOTE TO READERS: This book has been written and published for informational and educational purposes only. It is not intended to serve as medical advice or to be any form of medical treatment. You should always consult with your physician before altering or changing any aspect of your medical treatment. Do not stop or change any prescription medications without the guidance and advice of your physician. Any use of the information in this book is made on the reader's good judgment and is the reader's sole responsibility. This book is not intended to diagnose or treat any medical condition and is not a substitute for a physician. This book is independently authored and published and no sponsorship or endorsement of this book by, and no affiliation with, any trademarked brands or other products mentioned within is claimed o°r suggested. All trademarks that appear in this book belong to their respective owners and are used here for informational purposes only. The author and publisher encourage readers to patronize the quality brands mentioned in this book.

To all of my teachers:
your knowledge and embodied wisdom are
the backbone of this book.

~

To that place within each of us that knows the way home.

Contents

Introduction

Wholehearted Greetings

I welcome you and all of your being to *The Somatic Therapy Workbook*. This book is a labor of devotion to our individual and collective embodiment. To our capacity to inhabit our bodies and our relationships with every awakened and enlivened cell of our beings. To our capacity to repair patterns of trauma that separate us from the safety of our bodies. This book comes from a desire to help people arrive home in their bodies as their inherent birthright and intended landing pad for life's experiences. It comes from my deep belief in our capacity to heal—a belief that our individual bodies and our collective body know how to find and orient toward innate pathways for healing. Although this may not always look pretty or feel fantastic, it is possible to lean into the currents of health and aliveness that carry our bodies and psyches toward greater ease and well-being when we stop fighting the rapids of emotional and sensory experience and instead make way for what is happening in each moment.

Somatic practices ground us in our bodies as they are, not as they could or should be or as we wish them to be. It is from this platform of feeling into *right now* that we build a bridge between our mind, our body, and our heart. Engaging in somatic work is about becoming an integrated human organism: an organism that is inclusive of all parts of itself; an organism with healthy and coherent boundaries; an organism that has the capacity to reorient time and time again toward health and ease; an organism that can recover from overload and trauma—not just one that copes, holds on, and maintains hyperalertness for safety and survival. In this way, somatic practices are inherently healing and stress relieving and guide us toward well-being. Similarly, somatic practices, when applied therapeutically, are pivotal in the gritty work of trauma healing and repair.

Whom This Workbook Is For

This workbook is for all who are interested in exploring and developing their body-mind-heart relationship. It provides somatic and embodiment concepts and practices to nurture your whole being. You may find this work healing, supportive, inspiring, evocative, curious, integrating, and much more. This workbook is intended as a stand-alone guide to the principles of somatic psychology and somatic therapy and as a guide through your own somatic fabric to foster your healing and well-being. It is also intended as a companion guide for those engaged in any therapeutic work who may be looking for body-centered approaches; for movement practitioners seeking guidance in the emotional and psychological components of embodied movement practice; and for teachers and therapists seeking inspiration and, perhaps, a complementary journal-like tool to offer those whom they serve.

For those of you who are new to the world of somatic psychology and somatic therapies, may you discover more of yourself in these pages. For those of you already deeply invested in the work of somatics and somatic therapy, may you be reinspired and supported here. For those who are here to learn for yourselves, enjoy these inquires with great curiosity. For those passing these concepts and exercises along, thank you, and may this book serve the work you already do. For all of us, may this workbook and the practices within it be a light in our process of embodiment and sovereign health.

Engaging with the Workbook

Broken into three parts, this book offers a mix of conceptual and experiential theory, stories from my life and practice, experiential somatic and creative practices for your healing and well-being, and places for reflection on your ongoing process. Part 1 presents important terms and concepts in the world of somatics and background on the various streams of somatic therapies. Part 2 offers a look at the core principles shared across modalities of somatic psychology and somatic therapy. The presentation of each principle includes theory, story, and several practices to engage that theory. In Part 3, you will dive into practices to ignite your embodiment, enhance your mind-body-heart connection, and support your own growth and self-healing.

These three parts build on each other, offering you context, giving you the opportunity for lived experience, and providing you pathways to continually drop into the work, refine, deepen, reflect, and integrate. Although I recommend, at least initially, working through the book in the order it is offered, it is also useful to select the themes you'd most like to explore and skip around in the chapters, trusting your instincts for engagement.

Expectations and Limitations

This workbook is by no means an exhaustive review of the fields of somatics, somatic psychology, or somatic therapy. It is intended to be digestible in its scope and content. Think of it as a dip into the vast sea. You will explore experientially, for your own self-healing and well-being, the most universal principles shared across somatic therapy modalities.

All of the exercises and prompts are, of course, invitations, not definitive and singular ways to engage with the principles presented. You can certainly come up with your own creative ways to explore the various theories. Please use this as a springboard for your continued learning, and keep developing and improvising! If something just feels off to you, or is met with massive amounts of resistance, set it aside for the time being and come back later.

Always take good care of yourself while engaging the practices offered in this book. If thoughts, images, or feelings become too big or overwhelming for you to be with on your own, please seek safe consult. When an exercise prompts you to look at something potentially triggering, please stay close to a mild level of intensity as you work to build more bandwidth. Or choose to do the exercises with a therapist or mentor you trust. As you work with and move your body, attend to your physical safety and do only what feels appropriate and healthy. Modify the movement practices in accordance with your physical boundaries and needs. I am an able-bodied writer, practitioner, and teacher and am aware of that bias and limitation as I offer you these practices. I have, in many places, offered various ways to engage in the movement exercises so that both those who are highly mobile and those who have more constraints can find ample opportunity here.

This workbook is not intended to serve as psychotherapy, nor are any diagnoses attempted or implied in these pages. In my opinion, there is no replacement for psychotherapy. Though, for a variety of reasons, individual psychotherapy can be daunting or simply inaccessible for some. This is a workbook from which you may certainly gain psychotherapeutic benefit. Moving and breathing with conscious awareness—deepening your capacity to be present with your inner life—is always beneficial. Many of the somatic therapies explored in these pages are inherently therapeutic physically, psychologically, and emotionally. You may find you are finally ready to engage in psychotherapy after using this book. You may find this a useful companion to your already present therapeutic relationship. You may find this a journal to support your mind-body practice. Most of all, stay curious and trust yourself and your body. Deep trust and ample curiosity mixed with healthy relationships to our emotions can really go a very long way.

PART 1

The Somatic Therapy Landscape

CHAPTER 1

Terms and Context

As we begin this journey together, let us consider a few key terms to establish our collective vocabulary: *embodiment*, *soma*, *somatics*, *somatic psychology*, *somatic therapy*, and *somatic psychotherapy*. You may already have a notion of what these terms mean, both in their definitions and in what they mean to you personally. Take a moment here to write down your current understanding of these words. How do you define them based on your knowledge and experience? What do they mean to you? What is your experience with each of them? What are the differences between them, and how do they overlap and intersect?

EMBODIMENT:

_____

_____

_____

_____

SOMA:

_____

_____

_____

_____

SOMATICS:

_____

_____

_____

SOMATIC PSYCHOLOGY:

_____

_____

_____

_____

SOMATIC THERAPY:

_____

_____

_____

_____

SOMATIC PSYCHOTHERAPY:

_____

_____

_____

_____

Let's look a little more specifically now. Perhaps some of the following explanations will refine, clarify, enhance, or affirm your current understanding.

Embodiment

Embodiment describes the experience and process of fully inhabiting your skin in such a way that your thoughts, actions, feelings, and intentions find a cohesive expression through your body. It is when you unequivocally exhibit and represent that thing you are describing. When we say someone is the embodiment of grace, we might be referring to the way they are inhabiting their movements, speech, and qualities of life. Embodiment is how you take your insides and show them on your outside. Embodiment looks like allowing life to impact you and expressing that impact in clear ways. It is about feeling your own aliveness in your skin through sensations as you move through the world. Embodiment is about staying present internally while experiencing life. It is the experience that occurs when you are simultaneously aware of yourself inside your body, of the world around you, and of how you are experiencing them.

Embodiment, Dissociation, and Trauma

Embodiment is the antithesis, and therefore antidote to, dissociation, the phenomenon of vacating one's bodily experience as a result of overwhelm, stress, and trauma.[1] Dissociation is a rather normal response to trauma. It serves to protect you from feeling any more pain than is necessary. Trauma occurs when an event or a relationship dynamic overwhelms your nervous system to the point of massive reactivity for survival.[2] Dissociation is one of its hallmarks and can become an ingrained stress response so that even once the original threat has passed, this unconscious survival tactic plays out.[3] At the time of impact, dissociation protects your system, but over time this pattern of splitting and cutting off can become a recurrent and perpetual lived state that is unsatisfying at best and harming at worst. Patterns of dissociative behavior play out in our addictions, routines of self-medicating, and general disconnect from our bodies.[4]

The opposite of dissociation is embodiment—inhabiting your lived experience totally and fully. In this way, the path of embodiment is rather humbling. It is a path that requires your presence and fortitude to be impacted by all of life, not just by what is pleasant. Embodiment is a path that takes life on life's terms and hones our capacity to stay connected to ourselves and the world around us even when it is unpleasant, scary, dull, overloaded, and everything in between. Embodiment's best friend is presence, and together they cultivate the conversation of your ability to stay awake and attend to the experiences inside your skin while you are moving through life.[5] This is one of the primary reasons we know that embodiment helps repair traumatic experiences. Stress, overwhelm, and trauma send us outside of our bodily homes.[6] The unwinding of trauma must therefore include the body—your body. This reorienting to the home of your body is a process of embodiment.

Even if you have not incurred serious trauma, consider that embodiment is actually good for you. There is a common notion that avoiding negative experiences and compartmentalizing ourselves to separate from what we dislike is easier. This is why we see the rising tide of addiction, self-medicating, avoidance of true feelings, and lack of emotional vocabulary. Being present in your own skin actually helps you process and digest experiences more efficiently.[7] Instead of thinking about things, you can feel and respond in coherent ways. It helps you stay connected to what is true in your mind and heart, and it provides pathways for that expression so that emotions, experiences, and responses do not get stifled or truncated. In this way, I suggest to you that embodiment is actually stress relieving and innately tied to increased well-being. Or perhaps a better way to put it is that the very exercises and activities that we engage in to move toward embodiment are stress relieving and encourage our well-being: Slowing down. Pausing. Consciously breathing. Feeling our skin. Moving in ways that are not just routinized and are instead endlessly authentic. Allowing ourselves to feel fully.

Soma

In Greek, *soma* means "of the body." In English, it is defined as "the body of an organism,"[8] and in Sanskrit, it translates to "the nectar of immortality."[9] Soma, your soma, is the organism of your body and all the intelligence of experience it holds. It is the fabric of your being—threading your experiences through the organism of your body. Soma is the vessel through which you give and receive life. It holds your emotions and expresses your thoughts and habits. You are made of soma, and you are soma itself.

Somatics

Somatics is the study and practice of exploring and understanding the fabric of your soma through your internal awareness.[10] Somatic practices include movement and meditative techniques that invite you into a deep awareness of what it feels like to be inside your own skin as you inhabit it, whether in motion or in stillness. Somatic practices develop your embodiment and awareness—your *proprioception*, how your body moves in space, and your *interoception*, the experience of your body's internal sensations and movements.[11]

Methods can include attention to the quality of your breath during movement. What it feels like to move inside your body while you move, make shapes, and shift your body weight. What it feels like to experience being in your body as it gives and receives in the world. Somatics, in this way, is really the study of experiencing yourself in and through your own embodied living.

Somatic Psychology

Christine Caldwell, one of the pioneers in the theory and practice of contemporary somatic psychology, defines the field as "the study of the body-mind connection. It draws upon philosophy, medicine, and other sciences in an attempt to unify human beings into an organic whole for the purpose of healing and transformation."[12] The robust field of somatic psychology has a wide lineage base and draws upon various somatic modalities, traditional talk therapy techniques, neuroscience, attachment theory, and trauma healing to approach the health and healing of one's entire system. Looking at the individual as a whole organism means that one's body and mind are not separate. Rather, they are woven together intricately in the ways our thoughts and emotions express outwardly, how life events and opportunities impact our movement repertoires, how our unconscious manifests somatically, and how somatic awareness can reveal the unconscious to us.

Somatic Therapy

Somatic therapy is the application of somatic (body-mind) techniques for repair, integration, and healing at the biomechanical, physiological, neurological, and motor coordination levels. Somatic therapies address issues of the body such as motor delays, neurological impairment and decline, movement repatterning, and physical trauma to the body, as well as issues of the soma such as psychosomatic symptoms of stress and disease. Interventions can include gross and subtle movement, visualization, focused breathing, bodywork, and visceral manipulation. These interventions also affect the emotional and psychological health and development of the individual, which is inherently therapeutic and often psychotherapeutic.[13] The key here is that the inroad for somatic therapy is primarily for healing at the physical level that may then affect the mind and emotions.

For example, yoga may easily be considered a somatic therapy. The various techniques of the yoga postural practice work specifically at the layer of the physical body to create imprints in the deeper layers of one's being and consciousness. We do not consider going to yoga class the same as going to a therapist, but there is much truth to a saying I hear often, "Yoga is my therapy." Often people find that by utilizing body-centered practices to facilitate the conversation between their lived experience of physical expression, their thought patterns, and their emotions, a kind of well-being and overall health emerges.

Repair often occurs in and through these practices without one sitting in a psychotherapy office. We might say that all somatic therapies provide healing to undernourished, undersupported, and sometimes wounded places within, yet the overarching approach is to work directly with the physical body—muscles, bones, fascia, breath, motor coordination, and movement—with a potential benefit of psychological and emotional shifts.

Somatic Psychotherapy

Much like somatic therapy, *somatic psychotherapy* addresses the body-mind fabric toward healing and repair where needed. The inroad here is facilitating the health, repair, and healing of psychological, emotional, and developmental needs and traumatic experiences. Much like any psychotherapeutic model, which is really about healing places of abuse, trauma, neglect, distrust, and emotional dis-ease of all kinds, somatic psychotherapy offers this kind of healing but does so somatically—directly through the body.

Methods of somatic psychotherapy utilize various body-centered techniques to support the psychological health, healing, wholeness, and well-being of the individual.[14] Particular attention is focused on places where one's psychosocial-emotional development may have been interrupted or wounded,[15] as well as repairing wounds rooted in relational attachment[16] and, of course, trauma-related wounds and their respective symptoms.[17] Another hallmark of somatic psychotherapy is its focus on the nervous system as an embodied function and experience.[18] Thus, somatic psychotherapy implements interventions that ignite individuals' capacity to rewire their nervous system reactions into healthy responses, thereby generating a new embodied experience.

A somatic psychotherapy intervention might look like utilizing movement to physically execute a behavior that was repressed or dismissed during the impact of a traumatic event. When finally allowed to emerge and sequence through one's body, this expression brings relief and creates a new pathway of health within one's system.[19] Somatic psychotherapists might also explore a bodily sensation as a means to access deeper emotional awareness and literacy in relationships and responses to life events.[20] Practitioners often assess psychosocial-emotional development through the structures and contours of posture and movement and utilize sensory awareness and movement to foster developmentally appropriate growth.[21]

Overlapping Approaches

There are many areas in which somatic therapy and somatic psychotherapy overlap. For the purposes of this workbook, I encourage you to not get bogged down by these intricacies and subtle differences but instead to move through the content at your own pace with a mindset of self-healing for your soma. As a somatic psychotherapist, I am oriented toward the developmental, psychological, and emotional places of need in my clients. I listen and look for where this might be showing up in their bodies' movements, gestures, and felt experiences, and I help them use the direct experience of their bodies to support their psychological and emotional repair and health. As a somatic movement therapist and educator, which includes predominantly my work as a yoga teacher and free-form movement guide, I work directly with movement and physicality to support health in my clients' bodies and nervous systems. If and when emotional and psychological content emerges, I encourage and support their bodies to hold the experience as it unwinds. The difference here is really offering them resources and support rather than processing the material together as we do in psychotherapy. Yoga, 5Rhythms, and Authentic Movement, for example, are all somatic practices that can be applied therapeutically to support physical, emotional, and psychological well-being. Although they may not be psychotherapy per se, we may call them inherently therapeutic.

In a culture that is device-driven, fast-paced, predominantly sedentary, and focused on how efficiently our minds can process information and produce, embodiment and somatics offer us a return to our birthright of living inside a body. These practices require slowing down, paying attention, breathing consciously, and turning away from the screen and into the wild inner terrain of our selves. Whether this is done on one's own or with a safe other as a witness, the invitation into somatic practice is an invitation to return to the joy, fear, and humility of being in a body, of being a body, of being a human being. The more we can stay connected to our soma—to our somatic experience, to our innate wealth of health in our breath—the more we can reorient when things are difficult, return to the source of resilience within, and emanate that into our world. If embodiment is our birthright and soma is what we are made of, then it makes sense that we would use a practice rooted in the body to provide therapeutic intervention and change when needed.

CHAPTER 2

Forms and Modalities

The practices in this workbook draw from various sources and approaches across the rich landscape of somatic psychology, including body-mind practices, such as yoga and qigong; somatic movement practices with therapeutic benefits and applications, such as Body-Mind Centering, Authentic Movement, 5Rhythms, and the Focusing Technique; and somatic or body-centered psychotherapy, such as Body-Mind Psychotherapy, Sensorimotor Psychotherapy, and Somatic Experiencing. In this chapter you will find information about the various forms of somatic therapies and a brief history of somatic practice as a backdrop for the work of this self-guided book.

Plenty of discourse exists delineating the various forms of somatic practice and therapeutic application. I will not attempt to give you all of them here but will offer some guideposts. Christine Caldwell outlines the many therapeutic applications of somatics in her book *Getting in Touch: The Guide to New Body-Centered Therapies*.[22] She takes readers through key modalities of somatic psychology in support of their garnering a greater understanding of the landscape but also in finding a method for them to utilize in their own healing path. In *Mindful Movement: The Evolution of the Somatic Arts and Conscious Action*, Martha Eddy takes readers through various approaches to and vast benefits of somatics, including the rich history and influences of the field of somatics and related applications.[23]

Categories within Somatic Psychology

Somatic Practices and Arts   **Somatic Therapy**

Authentic Movement

5Rhythms

Open Floor

Qigong

Alexander Technique

Body-Mind Centering

Feldenkrais Method

Yoga

Bioenergetics

Clinical Somatics

Kestenberg Movement Profile

Network Spinal Analysis

Reiki

Rolfing Structural Integration

Yoga chakra theory

Body-Mind psychotherapy

Dance movement therapy

EMDR
(eye movement desensitization and reprocessing)

Hakomi Method

Moving Cycle

Sensorimotor psychotherapy

Somatic Experiencing

**Somatic Psychotherapy
and Dance Movement Therapy**

When I consider the world of somatic psychology, I delineate the field into three main categories: somatic practices and arts, somatic therapy, and somatic psychotherapy and dance movement therapy. *Somatic practices and arts* serve the development and awareness of the soma through movement, embodiment, and expressive arts. *Somatic therapy* includes embodiment- and movement-based practices to support the repair, healing, and expansion of developmental motor skills and movement repertoire. Manual and movement-oriented techniques are also used to restore and support the physical body. *Somatic psychotherapy and dance movement therapy* incorporate one's body, one's embodied experience, and one's movement impulses and expressions to understand and heal psychological, emotional, social, and developmental wounding and gaps.

Some of these modalities overlap categories to serve one's ongoing practice of embodiment and provide therapeutic support. Remember that a distinguishing factor between somatic therapy and somatic psychotherapy is whether a practice modality may have inherent healing or reparative potential and benefit or whether it is being used to support a psychosocial-emotional process rooted in developmental need or trauma. The chart on page 23 lists specific practices delineated by category. Again, we'll draw on various principles and practices across all these modalities in our work here. If a particular practice or category of practices intrigues you, use this chart as a resource to gather more information. Note the practices that share categories.

PART 2

Core Principles of Somatic Therapy

CHAPTER 3

Your Body Speaks through Sensations

Growing up, I learned about sensations from the perspective of sports and structured dance, in very much a *do this and you will feel that* sort of way. I was mostly aware of my inner world through what I could or couldn't do with my body, and my awareness of sensation was directly related to my physical capacity. It wasn't until I began practicing yoga and 5Rhythms, and later studying somatic psychology in graduate school, that I became deeply acquainted with and attuned to my inner sensory world. The idea that I could pay attention to my internal state and be in a relationship with my world was a bit foreign. It was a deep wonder for me to realize that I had within myself a vast landscape filled with feeling and sensory information, and that I could live rooted and connected to the thread of my inner awareness through sensations.

Because of my lack of sensory breadth and depth beyond structured form, I always felt a little outside my skin, as if I were watching myself trying to be myself, telling my body to do things instead of feeling it exist in the world as myself. I cannot pinpoint the exact moment I began living this way—a bit outside my body—but I can tell you with conviction that I live fully in my body now. Perhaps that is the true gift of recovering our innate sensory awareness capacity—we get to fully inhabit our bodies, for better or worse. In my experience, my sense of personal embodiment is directly connected to my awareness of my internal sensations. Of course, this has a sticky and painful neurotic edge, where one can get lost in one's internal state and be overwhelmed by the information within. I have gone to those dark places. Some of you have likely made yourselves totally strung out in your own internal obsessions too.

Now I can tell when I am disconnected and floating outside myself. I can actually feel it. And I can feel the experience of being down in my feet and all the way in my guts. It is from this attunement that I aim to live my life, make decisions, sit with clients, and raise a child. When I engage in physical activities, I am in a listening conversation of sensation. When I am cooking, I pay attention to what my body feels like. When I am in a tough conversation, I take time to return to what my body is speaking to me. I notice the heat and my heartbeat. I feel how my weight shifts and how my spine feels.

One of our goals here is to help you do just that. The safest place on Earth is actually your body, despite previous traumas, despite its constant growth and change, even despite the fact it will eventually decay. The Irish poet and philosopher John O'Donohue wrote, "Attunement to the senses can limber up the stiffened belief and gentle the hardened outlook. It can warm and heal the atrophied feelings that are the barriers exiling us from ourselves and separating us from each other."[24] Sensory awareness, regardless of your physical capacity or intricacies, is your birthright. Inside the fabric of your skin and bones, inside the organs and fibers of matter that make you, is a nonverbal language of understanding and communication always available to you. This is the language of sensation. Sensations are your body's way of communicating the unseen inside yourself directly to you. "Sensations are the language of the reptilian brain,"[25] wrote Peter Levine, creator of somatic experiencing in *Waking the Tiger*, a seminal and experiential book on healing trauma. They are the nonverbal language of your inner world, offering clues to your real-time felt experience and patterns of traumatic reactivity. One of my mentors in graduate school, Leah D'Abate, said that "sensations are unarguably true." My mentor Melissa Michaels, author of *Youth on Fire: Birthing a Generation of Embodied Global Leaders*, always described sensations to me as "the visceral experience of your aliveness." Your experience of sensations is personal and unique and tells you that you are alive. As such, your sensations take you deeply into your experience in the here and now. Sensations are how your inner world speaks to you. Awareness of them brings your insides into your conscious awareness.

Sensations indicate physical needs such as hunger and thirst, they indicate arousal and desire, and they can be markers of your emotional states as well as intuitive "gut feelings."[26]

Specifically speaking, sensations are descriptive words, such as *hot, cold, pinching, tingling, rough, smooth, fluid, tight, open*. For example, maybe you notice your belly feels tight, or your throat feels scratchy, your voice feels resonant, or your back feels hot. All of those are the sensory awareness of your body.

All of us have access to a sensory world. The building block for this awareness was present at birth, when we cried out in discomfort and arousal because of hunger, fatigue, and other needs. At this basic level, noticing and acting on sensory information is how we are designed. Since our culture generally lives in a fast-paced, highly mental mode, we often pay little attention to our body's experience. If you are reading this book, you likely already have a desire to know more about how deeply connected your body, mind, and emotions all are. Returning home to your body requires the capacity to actually *live* inside your skin. Being with your internal sensory experience roots you in your skin while you engage with your relationships and your world.[27] In this chapter, you will explore ways to identify sensations in your body—to reclaim an internal literacy. You will learn how to sense inwardly what is happening inside your tissues and, without judgment, to name them simply. The first and primary key principle within somatic therapy is this building block:

Your body speaks through sensations.

Flooding

For many people, especially those who have experienced shock or trauma through which they learned their body is an unsafe place to live, diving into the sensory world within themselves can be frustrating, scary, or, honestly, downright triggering. Perhaps you are already well acquainted with your internal states or are comfortable breathing and being in your own skin. For those of you who may feel trepidatious about this kind of work or find that as soon as you close your eyes and feel inside, you experience overwhelm or get flooded with information, slow things down and start where you are instead of diving all the way in right away.

When you get flooded with sensory information or immediately come upon a blankness inside, it is useful first to open your eyes and shift to holding a soft gaze. While you do this, simply bring your attention to the boundary of your skin. You do not need to go inside and dig around unnecessarily. Become aware of the feeling of your clothes on your skin, or the couch, or floor, or blanket beneath you. Simply feel what is touching your skin. Start here, coming into closer contact with the boundaries of your skin and what it feels like before going inside the boundary of your skin. You can place your hands on your belly or your face and feel your hands touching your own body, your own contact with yourself. Feel the ground beneath your feet and notice the sensations there.

You may need to practice in this way for some time—just bringing sensory awareness to the level of your skin in relationship to your own body and what's most immediately around you. This is excellent work. This gentle practice of sensing your skin and what is contacting it is useful with folks for whom it's just too much at first. If you are a yoga teacher or movement professional and you notice that students are getting a little overwhelmed by your invitations to internal awareness, use this practice of sensing the skin to slow down.

Numbness

For some, turning inward to sensations in their body is met quickly with a feeling of numbness. Clients and students will report that they "don't feel anything," or that "it's just blank in there," or that they "feel numb." Often this numbness arises when one has been excommunicated from their body and their birthright of having a sensory life. They are cut off from feeling their own aliveness inside. They are frozen and locked away from the flow of sensory language. And this is probably for good reason. Internal numbness to sensations is a response to shock and trauma.[28] This could be the result of experiences such as sexual abuse, addiction, or other relational dynamics in which one has been exposed to and marinating in toxicity that makes the experience of being in one's body unsafe. It is always important to treat this kind of understandable resistance to feeling internally with the utmost respect. Never force something to open that is not ready. The path here, as when getting flooded, is to slow down and thaw gently.

Consider that numbness is indeed a sensation. If you can identify that feeling of nothingness, blankness, or numbness, it is possible to sense and feel other sensations as well. If you come up against numbness, blankness, or the feeling of nothing, try the work with sensing your skin as a skill builder for developing a relationship to your sensory capacity.

If you turn inward and notice a sense of numbness somewhere in your body, bring your attention right to it in a loving way. You can actually befriend the numbness you feel, as with the way a dear friend would offer comfort to you when you are sad or angry. Crawl up next to the sense of numbness and internally say hello. Next, bring your breath to the part of your body that feels numb or blank. Imagine that body part has a pair of lungs. Breathe into that part fully and pay attention to any changes that occur. Even if that part remains closed or resistant for now, you are inviting your attention to knock on the door. Over time, as you begin to trust your experience more, the numbness will thaw, and more sensory life will come to full color.

Movement Exercise:
Body Scan to Identify Sensations

In this exercise, you will come into contact with your inner world through a simple body scan. You will go sequentially through your body, bringing your awareness to each body part, and notice what is happening sensorially inside. When you do this on your own and get proficient at turning inward, you can begin with any part of your body, but for now, let's start at your feet and work upward. I personally relish quietude, so I recommend finding a quiet spot to do this. That said, if some kind of soft, soothing music suits you to help you relax and drop in, then by all means play your favorite tunes for about ten minutes.

Sit comfortably or lie on the floor. Close your eyes or hold a soft, gentle gaze several feet out in front of you. First, just notice your natural breath for a minute. Sense its natural rise and fall. If at any time you have the impulse to bring your hands onto a part of your body, trust that completely.

Bring your attention down to the bottoms of your feet. You can wiggle your toes or jiggle your feet for a minute to land there. Notice what your feet feel like. Maybe the soles are tight or your toes feel tingly. Notice your ankles, and feel what your ankle bones are like inside right now. Let your attention rise to your calves and lower legs. What sensations are present there? Tightness or heat? Do your shins feel heavy? Now notice what your knees feel like internally. Maybe they are achy or crunchy. Bring your attention to the backs of your legs. What do you become aware of in the backs of your legs?

Remember, there should be no judgment at any point in this practice. You are simply becoming more deeply aware of the internal sensory life of your whole body, building a vocabulary and literacy from within.

Notice the fronts of your legs now. What are you aware of in your legs? Heaviness? Lightness? Let your attention move to your hips, noticing what it is like to bring your full attention there. What is arising? Breathe there and notice. Scan into your tailbone, sacrum, and lower belly. If you bring your breath there, what happens? What do you notice inside this part of your body right now? Bring your attention to your lower back; what do you notice there? Heat or cold, pressure or softness? Move up to your belly, feel into your belly, and allow your breath to show you sensation. Hunger. Gurgling. Fullness. Emptiness. Feel into your ribs and diaphragm and see what it's like in there.

Now notice your whole spine. Feel into each vertebra with care, and pay attention to how it feels. Now sense the front of your chest and feel what's going on in there. What happens around your metaphoric heart center when you bring your awareness and attention into your chest?

Feel into your throat with your awareness. What does your throat feel like today? Scratchy or smooth? How about the back of your neck? Feel the muscles along the back of your neck and notice what it feels like today. Pay attention to the sensations of aliveness in your arms, from your shoulders down into your elbows and all the way down into your hands and fingers. What catches your attention? What arises through sensation to the surface of your consciousness here?

Now bring your attention to your head. How does your head feel today? If you are lying down, notice the weight of your head on the floor. If you are sitting, let your head soften down toward your chest and notice its gravity. Sense around the top of your skull and bring your breath there. What does that feel like?

Now that you have scanned your body sensorially, take some deep, full breaths and visualize your body as one full organism. A whole vessel. Take full-body breaths for a moment. Finally, bring your hands to your belly and feel your hands contact your body. If your eyes are closed, open them; if they are in a soft gaze, sharpen your focus to come out of this body-centric meditation of sensation.

Write down any important findings from your sensory meditation below. Were you surprised? What caught your attention? How do you feel now after spending some time within? There are no right or wrong answers here, just some truth about your own experience of your body.

_____

_____

_____

_____

Journal Inquiry:
Build a Sensation Words List

Generate a list of as many words as you can describing sensations in your body: ones you have noticed in your body as well as other descriptive words for sensations that come to mind. Remember, sensations are the language of your felt sense and inner awareness. Find as many words as you can to build that vocabulary here. When you discover a new one, add it to your list.

_____ _____ _____

_____ _____ _____

_____ _____ _____

_____ _____ _____

_____ _____ _____

Drawing Exercise:
Express Sensations from the Inside Out

This exercise is intended for you to take what you sense internally and put it onto paper. For the next few minutes, you will tune in to your sensory world and then spend some time drawing what arises.

Gather some crayons, colored pencils, or pastels and have them handy along with this workbook or other paper. Next, set a timer for three to five minutes. Sit quietly or lie down somewhere comfortable. Close your eyes or hold a soft gaze with your eyes open. Turn and tune inward.

First, notice your breath: simple in and out. Then allow your awareness and attention to scan your body, noticing what is going on inside. Remember, there are no right or wrong sensations in your body. Even uncomfortable ones are worth noticing and connecting to, even numbness. Do not let yourself get overwhelmed, flooded with internal sensory information. If that starts to happen, place your hands on your belly, take a big, deep breath, and feel your hands on your skin. Then return to what is happening inside. The aim is to identify just a few sensations inside your body, such as bubbling in your belly, softness in your back, pinching in your knee. Once that timer is up, you can set it again for another five minutes or so.

Now pick one of those sensations and let yourself draw that sensation onto paper. You can even draw what numbness feels like. Don't worry at all about what the picture looks like or what colors you choose. Simply allow yourself to translate what you felt inside onto paper, where you can see it.

Real-Life Engagement:
One Eye In/One Eye Out

Living in a listening relationship to your sensory world takes a bit of practice at first. As with most habits that need care and tending, you will likely find that you need to pause throughout the day and come back to your awareness of your sensory life in little spurts. *When you sit down to drink your morning tea or coffee, take a moment and feel the movement of your breath between sips. When you get into your car, pause and feel into your skin, noticing one unarguably true thing going on inside. When you run your child's bath, sit down next to the tub and feel your heart beating and the temperature of your body. While you are engaging in a conversation, stay connected to your sensory experience while maintaining presence with the other person.*

In graduate school, I honed an essential embodiment practice that somatic therapists call One Eye In/One Eye Out. This is the basic capacity to track your internal experience while moving through and engaging with your life. Think of it as casting one eye of your gaze toward your inner landscape while offering the other eye to the world around you or the person with whom you are interacting. The capacity to oscillate your awareness in this way supports your embodied presence. It may be difficult to do this at first. You may find you tend to stay very internally focused or that you are pulled outward by the world around you. The following prompts will support your One Eye In/One Eye Out practice in your daily life.

In Daily Moments. Come back to your sensory awareness at little moments throughout the day whenever you can remember to do so. Note the sensations you are able to identify by remembering to tune inward during the day.

During Activities. Practice staying connected to your sensory experiences while doing an activity. For example, the next time you are at the grocery store, as you walk the aisles and make your selections, stay connected to what is happening inside you. What do you notice inside your belly when you choose your vegetables? When you are at your child's soccer practice, pay attention to how your body feels while you sit there and watch. Practice being present with yourself and what you are witnessing in the world. Take some notes on how this sensation practice is going for you.

_____

_____

_____

In Challenging Moments. Practice connecting to your internal sensations when you are having a difficult conversation with someone. Notice one, two, or three internal sensations while you are talking with your spouse about a heated topic. Stay aware of what is happening internally when you are "in it" with your mom. The aim here is to stay rooted in your true and real visceral experience while connecting with someone, even when it's hard. Take notes on how that is and anything that catches your attention.

_____

_____

_____

CHAPTER 4

Your Body Speaks through Movement

One day I sat on my therapist's couch expressing how angry I was at my partner. Further, I was confused and frustrated that my partner did not seem to understand or take seriously how angry I was at him. "I can't believe he can't see how angry I am," I said. "My anger is not really being seen." I went on, "How come when I express anger, he seems to minimize it and not take me seriously?"

In that moment she stopped me and responded, "You do realize you are smiling as you tell me this, right?"

"Excuse me? Really?" I touched my face to see if she was right. "I'm smiling?" I reached for my face again and noticed that indeed the corners of my mouth were turned upward. I felt angry and hot inside. And I was smiling.

I sat back into the leather couch and let her reflection sink in. I realized in that deepening moment that my facial expressions and my emotional feelings and gestures were incongruent. I sat there quietly feeling into this uncomfortable discrepancy. I had always considered myself a rather honest person. It had not dawned on me that what I was feeling inside and what I was expressing with my body on the outside did not actually match.

Somehow, somewhere, I learned to temper my expression of anger through smiling. No wonder I did not experience being taken seriously when I expressed this emotion in an argument or heated debate. No wonder I wasn't really being heard. My experience was easily disregarded and undercut through the smile peeking through, seeming to say, "I'm angry, but not too much"; "I'm pissed, but it's okay."

This moment in therapy initiated a journey toward tracking my embodied experience in relationship to my movement expressions closely and relentlessly. I worked tirelessly to risk the vulnerability of matching my facial expressions to what I was actually feeling internally. As a result, I have indeed found I am more believable, more coherent and congruent. Now, of course, there are always situations in which no matter how concrete and congruent and honest we are, people cannot receive us. They minimize and disregard authentic emotion being expressed because of their own discomfort. Women and girls are often taught not to show anger in clear and authentic ways. It is not often culturally acceptable for a woman to be angry. So women and girls are taught to minimize its expression to maintain the status quo. Nonetheless, finding coherence and congruence in how we feel and what we express, so our bodies can be tools in sharing our worlds, is an important life skill in our emotional intelligence repertoire.

~

Movement is a powerful way to communicate without words, a mode of expression that is often lost or forgotten as we get older and become more verbally articulate. Your body is the tool for your expression. Nonverbal communication through movement and gesture is a vital and natural way of relating. It communicates your thoughts, habits, and feelings both consciously and unconsciously.[29] Honing your capacity for conscious nonverbal communication and deepening your awareness of unconscious nonverbal communication can expand your repertoire of feeling, emoting, expressing, and communicating. Unconscious movement may support or reflect your inner state before it even lands in your conscious awareness.[30]

Think of all the small gestures you make daily that communicate nonverbally: a simple wave to a neighbor; a raised eyebrow when someone cuts you off; turning toward your partner when you feel connected or turning away when you need space or feel a contraction and are not yet aware of it. You likely do this all day without even realizing it, through body language and attunement to your world. The way you make hand gestures when telling a story, adjust your seat at a dinner party, navigate through a crowd, or make a habitual movement such as sweeping your hair from your shoulders—all of these are your unconscious part navigating your world nonverbally.

Then there are ways in which you can consciously choose to express yourself through movement. Much of our conscious movement is functional.[31] For example, getting up off the couch to get a glass of water, picking up your child, and bending down to tie your shoes are coordinated movements that we ask our bodies to do. They can also be the conscious articulation of feelings and experiences. Somatic movement practices such as conscious dance, yoga, and 5Rhythms, for example, are ways of moving that shed the light of our conscious awareness on both the movements we choose to do voluntarily and those we find ourselves doing organically. Practices such as these allow you to build a repertoire of movement beyond just functional and utilitarian movements and into creative, evocative, and expressive ranges of your body-mind complex.

Asking your child to show you how their day was or how an interaction went is a way of encouraging the conscious use of expression through movement. Putting on music and letting your body move organically to digest and integrate your day is a great way to express yourself without words. Letting your true and authentic emotions arise in a conversation and allowing yourself to cry, or grimace, or smile completely are ways of bringing more consciousness to your subtle movement expressions. Paying close attention to what arises in your dance and yoga practices and moving the energy purposefully through your limbs and breath are all ways to nourish this capacity of conscious expressive movement.

Somatic psychology and somatic therapy support you in observing and refining how your body moves, both consciously and unconsciously, thereby encouraging healthy embodiment. Somatic therapists help you become aware of your movement patterns and habits, and the places where you might be frozen or lack full range of movement, and expand your repertoire of fully articulated movements, feelings, and expressions.[32] We do this by helping you become more attuned not only to gross motor coordination but also to more subtle sensory awareness and tracking. In somatic therapy, we deepen your conscious awareness of how your body moves in space, as well as how that movement both impacts your inner experience of yourself and the world and reflects your inner terrain expressed outwardly.[33] This gives you greater access to the unconscious or less conscious movement patterns you experience and express daily and provides you with more confidence in using your body as a tool for expressing your thoughts and feelings. When you look across the scope of somatic psychology and somatic therapy, you will find this essential principle shared by all modalities:

Your body speaks through movement.

Movement Exercise:
Show Instead of Tell

In this exercise, you can express your thoughts, your feelings, and anything you want to share through movement rather than words. Try to convey whatever truly wants to be told through your body rather than getting anything right or exact with words.

Find as private a space as possible. Sit or stand for a moment, and close your eyes. Tune in to your breath rising and falling. Soften your head toward your heart a bit so you do not need to hold up your head and thoughts so much here as you arrive in your body. Now, use these prompts to experiment with showing instead of telling.

Start small and brief. Use your body to tell the story of your morning. Imagine you are telling your friend about your morning. What happened, and how did it go? Was it frantic or slow? How did it leave you feeling? Show this person you are "speaking" to your morning just through movement, no words.

Try a little more. Now tell the story of your day to this friend. Express through movement and gestures what happened in your day and how it felt to be you. Take your time, and pay attention to how your body feels moving in space. There is no need to force anything to happen; this is a practice of allowing yourself to be here as you are and use your body to express. Notice the times you get stuck in your head, and drop back into your body by noticing your breathing. Then return to showing instead of telling whatever wants to be shared regarding your day.

Go a little deeper. Pick an event from your life to play with expressing in the ways you have just practiced. This might be your baby shower or wedding day, a graduation, or your first day of college. Truly, it can be any memory of an event that you would like to express. This is about telling the story, expressing the story, without narrative words.

In my opinion, when working on our own it's best to choose things no more intense than 7 or 8 on a 1–10 scale (1 as the least intense, 10 as the most intense). Once you have decided on the event you want to tell through your body, find a safe space that has enough room to move in. Do not be deterred if your space is small. It might be helpful to imagine telling this to a friend you love and trust. Or, if it feels best to simply tell the ether your tale through your body, have at it. Lighting a candle and saying a little prayer, something like "May my body share whatever it needs to about this time. May my story be told clearly through my body," can help to ritualize the space. (We'll get into more ways to ritualize these practices at the end of the workbook.)

Spend a moment sitting or standing with either a soft gaze or closed eyes, and tune in to the sound of your breath moving in your body. Notice whatever part of your body is making contact with the floor, and ground yourself there. When it feels just right, begin to move your body, showing instead of telling your story. Let yourself be surprised, allowing your body to share, express, and speak the narrative. As in the previous exercise, pay attention to your body's sensations and what is happening for you. If you start to get lost or feel stuck in your head and thoughts about it all, come right back to your breath for a pause. Then get back into it as you are moved.

As you move your body to tell your story, pay attention to how you are moving. What parts of your body move the most? Are there movements that you find yourself repeating? Are your movements large or rather small?

Journal Inquiry:
Write after Moving

Take some time now to cull your experience for insights from the movement practices you just tried. I recommend writing after each time you practice Show Instead of Tell, even if it's just a few words. After the exercise of showing your day, write down briefly what you noticed. Were you surprised by what came up? What did you notice in your body? How do you feel right now, having spent time moving your body as a tool for expression?

Drawing Exercise:
Draw What You Unearthed

Following your Show Instead of Tell practice, take a few minutes to draw. This will allow you to see reflected back to you some of what you unearthed in the movement, on paper. Don't worry if you are not much of an artist. That is not the point. You are not drawing anything specific; rather, this is a channel for free expression.

Set a timer for five to ten minutes. Pick up some pastels or crayons and draw whatever comes from inside you and through your hand. Colors, shapes, swirls, specific images all have free reign here as your unconscious comes onto the page. You may find that a specific image, color, word, or shape came up when you were moving. Put that down on paper here too.

Real-Life Engagement:
Congruent Expression

I wager that many of you have difficulty fully allowing yourselves to express what is really happening for you. Maybe, like me, you learned to temper your anger with a smile. Or perhaps you learned to apologize or lift an eyebrow in doubt to counter your certainty. Maybe you learned to smile only halfway or to slump your shoulders when you feel joy or excitement. Most of us have unconscious patterns of incongruence between our inner experience and our outer expression. Since embodiment is essentially about becoming more congruent and expressing as such to the outer world, it is often healing to dare and risk learning to match our insides with what we show on the outside.

Your real-world experiment here is twofold. The first part is to begin noticing when you are making a gesture with your body or face that is counter to how you feel inside. Take note. How does your posture shift depending on your mood? Do you temper or soften the expressions of your emotions by showing something else? Become conscious of the ways your body expresses.

The second part is bravely beginning to match your inner experience and your outer expression. If you notice that you smile when angry, try softening your face, taking a deep breath, and allowing your anger to move through your eyes, cheeks, and mouth. Allow your anger to show through your hand gestures and posture. Allow your body to express the story of your emotion. If you notice that you often temper your joy or excitement, use the same practice. Allow yourself to fully experience the emotion and show it through your posture. Let your smile and giggle shine. Jump, hop, be silly in your bodily gestures if it is true.

CHAPTER 5

Your Body Has Boundaries

A boundary is the space that distinguishes you from others. Practically speaking, you live a life contained within a body that is composed of elements that all work together as a system but are also unique entities unto themselves.[34] As a human being, you began life in utero—inside a sac floating in fluids. You developed inside the body of another human being, connected through the umbilical cord. The moment you were born, differentiation occurred, and you existed singularly for the first time. As a newborn and infant, you were dependent entirely on your caregivers for all of your needs. In this way, your first orientation to boundaries is with your parents and earliest caregivers.[35] When my daughter was born, she spent the first two weeks of her life naked on my bare chest. For much of her infancy she was attached to me. As she grew, the levels of contact between us shifted depending on her needs. One of the hallmarks of her development and differentiation is its consistent tethering toward her own sense of personal boundaries. Her ability to say no and yes and to come close or move farther away are all keys in her development as her own person. This also corresponds to her ability to accomplish tasks on her own as well as ask for what she needs.

Kinesphere

The notion of a kinesphere comes from Rudolf Laban's somatic movement and analysis technique, Laban Movement Analysis, a lens for viewing and interpreting movement. It denotes one's own personal movement space.[36] Your *kinesphere* is your movement and energy boundary. It is the space around you that belongs to you. It extends out just beyond your fingertips in every direction and plane of possible movement and gives the mover a sense of how far their movements and the energy of their movements can extend before bumping into another mover. As you move in the world, consider how you move not only within your skin but also within your kinesphere. Do you allow your movement and energy to really fill the whole space of your kinesphere? Which planes of movement do you habitually move within? What parts of your kinesphere are shadowed and neglected? Consider what happens when your kinesphere merges with another's and the difference that creates in movement.

When we talk about boundaries in somatic psychology and somatic therapy, we define them first at the very practical level of one's sense of boundary as a being living in a body. Inside this body of your skin exists a whole world unto you. This is your sovereign and holy space. Your skin houses your inner body, not just physically but also energetically.[37] Thus, your inner awareness is a rich garden of experiences. Somatic psychology also explores how bodies move within their own kinespheres and how they interact with one another[38]— how bodies move with or against each other, how they repel and attract and make new things together. This is as much physical as energetic. And it is culturally specific. In some cultures, more personal space is considered normal and appropriate. In other cultures, more closeness is the norm. The notion that individuals may retain their sovereign personal boundaries is dependent on the acculturation and gendering they have received as well.

Boundaries, Relationship, and Consent

Your sense of personal boundaries informs your capacity to give, receive, and honor consent.[39] In relationships, you negotiate the giving, occupying, and receiving of space and boundaries all the time. In places of boundary-crossing and violation, we feel agitated, hurt, disrespected, and overpowered. New contracts and healing must occur for the safety of boundaries to be reestablished. The feeling of merging with a partner or bonding with a child and having the intimacy that comes from individual boundaries dissolving a bit can be ecstatic. Whether boundaries yield closeness or establish distance, they are vital to our embodiment. They help us stay differentiated as ourselves with the capacity to connect consensually.

Boundaries are the containers within which all relationships occur; these include your relationship with yourself as well as your relationships with others. Examples of boundaries are personal space, commitments to time, and respecting space and belongings, energy, and nature. If the boundaries provided to you as a child were fuzzy or inconsistent, you may have internalized this relationship and then created ambiguous boundaries as an adult.[40] Recalibrating to a healthy sense of boundaries, in which you do not betray your own commitments and are able to articulate your boundary needs in relationships, is vital to healthy adulthood.[41] Somatic therapies utilize the felt sense of the boundary lines in your body to inform how you relate to boundaries in the rest of your life.

Somatic therapy cultivates, refines, and empowers your sense of boundaries at the physical level, the psychosocial-emotional level, and the relational level. The tools of moving, breathing, sensing, feeling—all of which you began exploring earlier in this workbook—build your ability to sense, identify, and stay connected to your boundaries, and to take action based on them. Somatic psychology and somatic therapy offer you this core principle:

Your body has boundaries.

Find and Explore Your Boundaries

Take some time here to explore, experience, and strengthen the sense of your boundaries inside your own skin. I find that when I have a clear and strong sense of boundaries internally stemming from a very basic and physical level, it translates to an ability to find rightful boundaries in my real-time relationships and choices. May these movement practices help you cultivate that too.

Movement Exercise:
Identify Your Physical Boundary

To explore the boundaries of your body, stand with your feet about hip distance apart and firmly placed beneath you. Softly bend your knees, just so you are not standing too rigidly. Place your hands on your body and breathe. Pay attention to the rise and fall of your breath moving into and away from your hands. Next, make fists or use your fingertips and begin tapping your body from head to toe. Tap over the entirety of your skin, starting from your head and face and neck, down the sides of your body and along your torso, then down the fronts and backs of your legs. When you have done this, stand with your arms by your sides and close your eyes. Feel the boundary of your skin. Notice the sensations of that boundary. Notice the energy along and underneath this surface.

Anytime you feel a bit spun out, feel disengaged from your body, or are having trouble maintaining contact with good and healthy boundaries, return to this exercise.

Movement Exercise:
Articulate the Boundary of Your Kinesphere

From this space of your awakened boundaries along your skin, explore your sense of personal space, your kinesphere. Remember, your kinesphere is the space around you that is just at the edge of an arm's reach. Imagine that distance making a sphere around you. This is your personal boundary space.

Step your feet wide apart from each other. Stretch your arms wide. Feel across the length of your arms and legs and take up space. Feel from inside your body to the boundary of your skin and then through your bones to the edges of your personal space. Repeat this, standing with your feet comfortably apart and reaching as fully as you can out in front of you, then above you. Continue to breathe and feel your body, both internally and in space.

Trace your kinesphere around you now. With your arms stretched up, turn one arm in a wide circle around you. Then do the same with the other arm. Envision and carve your sense of personal space with this motion. Imagine that a sphere or bubble surrounds you. Notice what it feels like to have a sense of this boundary of personal space. Feel what it is like to be present and inside your own personal space. If emotions arise, let them. Welcome this personal and intimate place where only you are.

Return to these practices of articulating the boundary of your skin and the sense of your boundary lines anytime you feel your internal awareness of boundaries or the way you are carrying them out in the world has become weakened. Even if your boundaries have been negated, trampled on, or violated in some way, it is possible to return to a strong and healthy sense of personal boundaries, both within your own skin and in the immediate and personal space around you.

Journal Inquiry:
Write from Your Boundaries

Using the previous movement practice as a springboard for contemplation, note any thoughts, feelings, and insights that arose from your boundary exploration.

WHEN I AM CLEAR ABOUT MY SENSE OF BOUNDARIES, I FEEL ...

_____

_____

_____

_____

THE PERSONAL BOUNDARY OF MY SKIN FEELS ...

_____

_____

_____

_____

DESCRIBE WHAT IT WAS LIKE TO IDENTIFY YOUR SKIN AS A BOUNDARY. WHEN, IF EVER, WAS THE LAST TIME YOU FELT THAT BOUNDARY AS CLEARLY?

WHAT WAS IT LIKE TO IDENTIFY AND CARVE OUT YOUR PERSONAL SPACE? WHAT HAPPENED INTERNALLY FOR YOU? WRITE DOWN ANY THOUGHTS OR FEELINGS THAT CAUGHT YOUR ATTENTION.

IF YOU HAVE EVER HAD YOUR BOUNDARIES VIOLATED, IGNORED, OR MADE UNIMPORTANT, SPEND SOME TIME WRITING ABOUT THAT HERE.

Creative Exercise:
Draw and Paint Clear Boundaries

I recommend using watercolors for this exercise if you have them. If you don't, fear not. Use paints you can water down, or even use pastels or crayons instead if needed. This exercise is a way for you to play with boundaries in an artistic form on paper.

Using any colors you like, paint the following types of boundaries by using different brushstrokes and shapes. Explore how it feels to put these to paper, and notice what you see reflected back to you in relation to the boundary work you have already done.

Blurry	Direct
Messy	On point
Unclear	Purposeful
Bleeding	Rigid
Faint	Intense
Muddy	Soft
Confusing	Open
Sticky	Fluid
Clear	Trustworthy

Real-Life Engagement:
Practice Your Boundaries

As mentioned earlier in this chapter, if you have a history of being disconnected from your personal boundaries, have had your boundaries violated, or were taught and modeled that boundaries were simply not allowed, staying connected to your sense of personal boundaries may be challenging. You might find you allow others to cross that inner line. You might find you do not even know yet where a boundary is inside yourself. You might find that your boundaries are outdated for your current life circumstances. Perhaps you want closeness where your pattern is to stay back. Perhaps you move too quickly to closeness instead of holding the challenging and often uncomfortable boundary instead. Remember, different relationships require different boundaries. Some relationships will have more firm and distant boundaries. Other relationships may have boundaries that are very close and even overlapping.

Learning to identify your boundaries, stay connected to them, and move through the world with them intact takes some work. Be patient with yourself. On some days and in some situations, you may find it is easier to stay with your boundaries; in other situations, it may be much more challenging. The key is to stay connected, aware, embodied, and willing to listen and engage the boundaries appropriate for you. Engaging in a personal space awareness practice can help you stay current with your boundaries at the very foundational and essential somatic level.

The next time you are waiting in line, pay attention to how close or far you are standing in relation to the people in front of and behind you. Does the closeness or distance you feel seem comfortable? Would you ideally like more space or less? How do you know? What arises in your body when you become aware of needing more space, if so?

You can track the same quality at a dinner party or any gathering. Treat this exploration as a little experiment with yourself. How close or far away do you like to be in relationship to people, and how does that change if they are a stranger, an acquaintance, a close friend, a partner, a child, a parent? Pay attention to what arises somatically for you around the sense of closeness or space.

The next step from this awareness is to dare to make the desired change. For example, if you feel too close, could you back up or ask the person to give you a little space? Sometimes it might be possible to identify our desired personal space, but it can be hard to ask. What happens when you actually speak your boundary out loud?

Use this work to also support you in identifying little boundary steps within you that are less physical and more about your needs in relationship. The same somatic markers that ignite when you physically need space will likely go off when other kinds of boundaries are being encroached upon. Perhaps you need space in a conversation. Or a time boundary needs to be honored. Or you have made a commitment to yourself that is hard to keep. All of these are boundaries for your relationships to yourself and those around you.

CHAPTER 6

Your Body Has Impulses You Can Trust

The foundation of human movement rests on physiological reflexes and innate desire.[42] Basic reflexes, such as the rooting and Moro reflexes and others visible in infant behavior, develop into increasingly complex motor actions such as rolling over, picking a ball up off the floor, crawling, walking, and running.[43] These mature into movement sequences and patterns such as swinging on monkey bars and doing a somersault. And, from there, into the possibility for expansive and spontaneous movement repertoires such as dance, yoga, gymnastics, soccer-field maneuvers, and all creative play.[44]

These motor sequences and movement patterns develop in tandem with one's instincts and impulses of need and desire.[45] Basic desire is linked to our essential needs for food, water, and connection. Newborns orient to their caregivers through scent and sound. Infants orient toward caregivers through eye gazing, crying, turning their head, or reaching toward what or who they want. Desire motivates new motor development. We learn to orient toward the things we need and want and to move in our world to get them.[46]

Together, these pathways become the interconnected constellations of your soma, from basic impulses and reflexes to developmental locomotive patterns to motor coordination and then movement repertoires.[47] In the context of the therapeutic application of movement, reflexes and impulses as the building blocks of movement indicate the complex weaving between motor development, movement repertoires, and psychological and developmental desires and needs.[48] Looking across the span of somatic psychology and somatic therapy practices, we find this principle encoded as a building block:

Your body has impulses you can trust.

Impulse, Desire, and Need

Have you ever had the impulse to reach out to a friend for a hug but stopped yourself? Have you ever had the desire to make that phone call but second-guessed yourself? Or noticed your hunger and ignored it? Have you ever had the urge to cry but stifled your tears to appear put-together or stoic? Or have you dampened your expression of joy to fit into the needs of a group, or held back anger out of fear of judgment?

I have yet to meet someone who does not relate to feeling their desire, impulse, and need and then finding themselves ignoring it or choosing to negate it. As infants and young children, we learn to navigate the charge and intensity of our needs. Depending on how these were or were not supported, we develop an internalized relationship to feeling the swells of impulse, desire, and need.[49] Some of us have learned to turn away from our needs. Others have learned to demand they be met by those around us. Or we may have adopted strategies to go out and take what we believe we need without considering the impact or consequences to those around us. Consequently these patterns are reflected in our motor sequences and patterned movement habits.[50]

We can look at movement impulses that may have been interrupted or truncated as a key to freeing up one's healthy desire, force of will, and connection to psychological and emotional needs.[51] Sometimes when I am witnessing clients, I notice repetitive movement patterns that arise as they speak and show emotion. Sometime these movement gestures seem to correspond to the content they are sharing. Sometimes it seems as though the gesture is cut short, like there is something underneath the surface of what is overtly being said and shown. It is as if the gesture holds a broader movement pattern living in their body that they curtail unconsciously. I often bring these movement tags—gestures that link to larger movements needing to sequence—to the client's attention.[52] I invite them to stay with what is happening inside and connect to how that movement truly wants to fully express. I encourage them to repeat the movement and explore exaggerating it, sometimes letting it move more completely through their soma. Tracking and expressing these movement tags often takes clients into a deeper awareness of their emotional state. It is an approach (or intervention) that facilitates the merging of bodily movement with present moment consciousness. They come into direct contact with the thought, emotion, and part of themselves that has also been interrupted when movement is truncated.

In this way, somatic psychology and somatic therapy are a direct invitation to explore how impulse, emotion, and gesture flow together. When a movement sequence is able to flow, contact with one's internal psychosocial-emotional state is felt and then freed up to articulate clearly. Tracking movement tags to free up blocked energy, truncated needs, and interrupted impulses deepens and widens the grooves of embodiment.[53] It is energetically and emotionally expensive to repress true need and desire, to shrink and make oneself smaller physically. Allowing what was previously limited to flow freely releases stored energy in all layers of our being. We integrate and become more congruent by untying the knots in the fabric of our soma.

The Satisfaction Cycle

This link between desire, emotion, and movement also means that in fostering our awareness and health in tracking our own desires and needs, we impact the way our bodies move through the world. There is a kind of confidence and presence that imbues one who is fully in ownership of their desire. They can say, "This is what I want and need. This is my request. This is me reaching toward what I need and receiving the satisfaction of its completion." This pattern, called the satisfaction cycle, illustrates a wavelike cycle within which we feel the impulses of desire rise, feel the movement toward meeting the need associated with it orient, and receive it fully into our soma, digesting its nourishment.[54] These stages in the cycle correspond to foundational motor movements:[55] yielding, which involves the ability to feel and sense; pushing, which is the orienting toward an object of desire; reaching, which is how we move toward that which we desire; grasping, which is how we take hold of that object of desire; and pulling, which is how we draw the desire toward us.

This cycle, formulated by Bonnie Bainbridge Cohen in her pioneering somatic work Body-Mind Centering and later expanded upon in relationship to psychological development by

Susan Aposhyan, describes the critical ways in which we orient toward what we need and want as the impetus for motor development, which later becomes our movement repertoire. In infants, we see this orientation in how they reach for their caregiver or a toy and in their motor development of rolling over, pushing themselves up, and crawling toward what they want. In children, we often see a kind of freedom in asking and reaching for what they want and moving toward it. As we get older, our relationship to the interconnectedness of our desire, impulse, and movement may become quite complex.

Trauma, social pretense, boundary violations, rejections, and shame all deepen our understanding of what happens when we act on our desire. If as a child you were not encouraged to follow your impulses, or you were constantly questioned or told to feel something else, your relationship to personal desire might have become quite strained. As we restore the presence in our own desire, we free up organic impulse, which then illumines greater movement, or at least the inner feeling of more freedom.

Viewing impulse and desire through the lens of movement and sensation can support you in a more easeful relationship with yourself and your world. If movement is a manifestation of your desire and impulse, use movement to restore healthy attunement to your needs, desires, and impulses where they have been forgotten, judged, interrupted, or truncated. Restoring your capacity in noticing impulse and desire can help you to trust and relax into your body's knowing. This can support you to take responsibility for your needs in constructive ways, ultimately allowing you to embody and take action toward your authentic desires in innumerable ways.

Movement Exercise:
Move from Impulse Rather than Thought

As adults we often move to do, rather than because we are. Of course, this way of being in the world is not bad. In fact, it is necessary. Yet it is also important to retain, or in many cases remember, your capacity to move from within. When you develop a steady practice of listening to your inner impulses, you come to find that movement can initiate from internal awareness and feeling, as opposed to only thinking about moving and then asking your body to move. The roots of this exercise are the moving meditation practice Authentic

Movement, created by Janet Adler and Mary Starks Whitehouse, among others. Here, you nourish and remember your innate capacity to move from impulse, not just thought.[56]

Find a comfortable space to move for a few minutes, free from distraction. Begin by standing, sitting, leaning against a wall, or lying down, anywhere that feels comfortable. In fact, trust your immediate impulse of where you'd like to begin.

Set a timer for five minutes. As you continue with this practice, you will add time. But for now, five minutes. Close your eyes and turn toward the experience of your breathing. You may find that placing your hands on your body helps you land your attention on what your breath is like right now. As a practice of allowing, begin to move. The movements can be big or small, subtle or large. You may simply notice movement inside yourself more than your body moving outwardly. If your mind goes into thinking, just come back down into the sensations of your body finding its own pathway of movement. The practice is in trusting whatever way your body naturally moves without the need to perform any task.

After completing this moving meditation practice, take a few minutes to write down what it was like for you. What surprised you about moving this way? What stood out to you? What felt like a way of moving that is habitual and common? What felt new and surprising?

Journal Inquiry:
Freewrite

Your invitation here is to freewrite, literally free write! Set your timer for seven to ten minutes. Without letting your pen leave the page, write continuously. Do not worry about the words and sentences making sense. Allow your immediate thoughts, feelings, insights, and impulses to come through you onto the page. Once you are done, go back and reread your words. Underline or highlight the words and phrases that jump out to you. Pay attention to any words or patterns than strike you, have impact, or bring up emotions or memories.

Creative Exercise:
Collage from Your Unconscious

I do not consider myself a massively creative visual artist. My forms of artistic expression are mainly writing and movement. Believe it or not, though, I really love to collage. I have collaged boxes of various sizes, boards, and shapes that I then cut out and made into objects and mobiles. You name it, I have likely collaged it. You will need anything that has images you can cut out and glue onto something. Think old magazines, papers, cards, the fronts of cards you have received, tissue paper from presents, and old calendars. You'll need those along with some glue and whatever surface upon which you will render the images. This could be an old shoebox, a mason jar, or a piece of cardboard. Your invitation is to let your unconscious speak through image. Abandon the idea of finding the right images, and allow the images to come to you, creating whatever they create. As with the other practices in this chapter, you are honing your capacity to move from impulse and intuition.

Find a comfy place to sit on the floor or at your table. Dump the magazines out and begin to flip through them. Tear or cut out the images that speak to you. Don't worry about what they are or what they potentially mean. Simply let the images entice you. Trust your impulse in being drawn to images you want to reserve for the collage. Once you have gathered a fair amount of material, begin to arrange them on the box or board. I find this an interesting practice; I am curious about how to fit certain images together or overlap them, how the placement of one color or shape or feeling expressed in imagery yields to the next. Your work here is to fully, and without judgment or criticism, let your unconscious move by attending to the images. Once you are done, let your collage dry, and consider what is being reflected back to you. Over time, you might find that an image makes sense in a new way or has a certain meaning.

Real-Life Engagement:
Spend a Day Moving from Impulse

Have you ever allowed yourself to go through your day doing only the activities you feel a healthy impulse to do? Most of us live our lives duty bound to our commitments, with pretty strict ideas about what we should or shouldn't be doing with our time, energy, and routines. When we have a history of denying our healthy impulses, we often shut down an important intuitive inner circuit that tells us our desires are good and healthy, can be reached for, can be met, and will be satisfying when they are met. As we explored earlier in this chapter, there are many places where this circuitry can get twisted or cut. Nourishing the roots of our basic impulses can be an enlivening real-life practice.

Recalibrate toward knowing and owning your impulses as healthy and okay by spending a day or two allowing yourself to basically do what you feel is right. Simply said, do what you want when you want. If you are rolling your eyes at this point and saying, "Oh yeah, I can't ever do that because I have to take care of the kids" or "I have a job!" or "I can't because __" (fill in the blank), I believe you. In real life and real time and with real responsibilities, we can't always do what we want when we want. And sometimes what we might desire is not the healthiest choice for us. This is not so much an exercise in enjoying a free-for-all as an opportunity to practice listening to what you need and desire as guidance for choices throughout the day. It is a practice in recalibrating healthy impulse. As we mature, we learn (we hope) to manage the urgency of our needs and desires. We learn impulse control so our boundaries can be upheld and we can respect others' boundaries too; we learn how to balance our needs with the needs of others. All of that is important and true. And yet it is also true that a little dose of doing what you want based on tracking your intuitive impulses can be deeply nourishing, especially if you are bound by the needs of others for much of the day. The following are ways you can practice trusting your impulses.

For one day, let yourself be guided solely by your healthy impulses. Don't overthink what your body is telling you. If you have cultivated the sensory awareness lessons in the earlier chapters, you are in a great position to attune and listen to your body as a guide to your impulses for your daily choices.

Stay connected to your hunger and thirst. Simply said, if you are thirsty, drink. If you are hungry, eat. Even if you feel hungry before it's "time to eat," just eat. Pay close attention to what it's like to eat when you are hungry. When you make your choices about what to eat, take a pause and see if there is something bubbling up in you that you would like to have. If not, directly ask yourself and your body. Honor what it says. You may surprise yourself.

When you make a choice about exercising for the day, pause before engaging in your normal routine. Ask yourself how you really want to move your body. Indulge in doing what you want! Maybe it's going to the gym when normally you do yoga. Maybe it's some light stretching instead of that run. Maybe it's skipping movement altogether in favor of journaling or resting or tending to your home.

Let yourself go to bed whenever you like, even if it means not finishing a project or feeling like a bit of a rebel and staying up late enjoying a movie or good book or company.

Pay particular attention to what it feels like to be in the flow of listening to and honoring your impulses as the way to guide you through your day. What is hard or uncomfortable? What is easy? Do you want more of this?

CHAPTER 7

Your Body Stores Information

Bodies are homes of information and experience. Like a tapestry woven from many exquisite threads, your life in your body is woven from your experiences, even the forgotten moments, and your learned and unknown lineage. Woven into the fabric of your soma are all of the positive, endearing experiences of your life, as well as those that were traumatic and painful. Your soma's texture includes the ancestral threads of lived experience passed down from previous generations into you. The joy, education, resilience, and survival of your ancestors are present as much as the places of trauma, oppression, neglect, hiding, and loss. The feelings associated with these experiences are also held within your body. Movement and somatic awareness serve to both generate this weaving process and repair holes in the fabric of your soma. They can serve to express these threads by evoking what has been forgotten and long unseen. They can support the frayed threads needing repair. Pulling on a thread of movement may tug a memory or a feeling. Pulling on a feeling may tug a movement sequence longing to be expressed.

Narratives, experiences, and patterns are imprinted through all the different layers and systems of your body.[57] The stories woven into your soma thread through your bones, muscles, marrow, fat, blood, and breath. To know the story of your whole being is to know the stories encoded in the different tissues and systems of your body. These systems include your muscular, skeletal, nervous, respiratory, circulatory, endocrine, and lymphatic systems as well as the fluids and skin.[58] Since your bones, muscles, organs, and tissues carry the imprinted memories of experience, when you engage in practices that stimulate these different systems, those stories can move to the surface to be reexperienced, looked at anew, and even healed.[59] Similarly, paying close attention to the felt sense of the different systems of your body through somatically oriented meditation and movement modalities can help you uncover and decode the embodied stories living within.[60] You can begin to remember long-lost stories of who you are, where you came from, and what you have experienced.

Somatic psychology and related therapies investigate the ways in which emotions, thoughts, and experiences are stored in the various systems of your body.[61] They utilize somatic awareness and movement to explore, express, and at times, repair the emotional, psychological, and even cultural information housed in the tapestry of soma. They also may emphasize the other direction: how the emotional and psychological experiences weave together the movements of your body to create your gestures, movement patterns, and expressions. Some modalities utilize these phenomena as means to create dance, poetry, and expressive arts. Regardless of the entry point, all forms of somatic therapy hold this core principle:

Your body stores information.

In both small and big ways, my body is the living, breathing, very much alive home of all my exposure to life itself as well as my inherited lineage: events I can consciously recall; the conscious and unconscious impacts of those experiences; the feelings associated with them; memories reaching into the deep caverns of my organs and tissues linking me to my grandparents in hiding during the Holocaust; intuitive knowings that live below the place of thought and "making sense," that reveal themselves through dreams and hunches or in chronic physical and sensory patterns.

I have had plenty of psychosomatic symptoms—physical sensations and ailments that somehow seemed structural in nature but at the root were tied to larger emotional currents embedded in my tissues and systems that needed support and expression. I have places in my body that consistently store fear or grief in specific ways. My bones and muscles tell the stories of car accidents, falls, my childhood and adolescence of figure skating. The memory of my child's exact moment of birth remains imprinted in my cells. I have come to emphatically trust the ways in which the various systems of my body are impacted by my life, gather and store information, and sometimes need support to release or weave the narrative of my soma in a healthier manner.

Movement Exercise 1:
Sense and Move from the Systems of Your Body

Embodiment and somatic well-being include awareness of the deepest layers of your living body. Inspired by Bonnie Bainbridge Cohen's Body-Mind Centering, as well as the work of Susan Aposhyan in *Natural Intelligence*,[62] this exercise is designed to help you bring somatic awareness to the various systems of your body. You can follow these prompts in the order presented here to create a full-body practice, or you can choose one at a time, exploring what speaks to you on any given day. As you sense into each system, you will build a conscious thread of awareness of it, as well as awaken to what arises within each system once the light of your awareness streams into it. Pay attention to the emotions, narratives, and beliefs arising from these moving meditations as well.

Cellular Breathing:
Your Body Is a Whole Organism

Lying on the floor, close your eyes and feel the full weight of your whole body. Feel yourself breathing. Ignite and expand your breathing through your whole body: the back and front and sides; down through your fingers and toes. Feel your whole body breathing as one organism. Now imagine that each cell in your body has a set of lungs and is breathing. Sense into your cells, expanding and contracting with each breath to ignite this kind of cellular breathing. As each cell of your body breathes fully and in harmony, your entire being breathes more fully.

Circulation:
Your Body Moves Blood and Oxygen in Its Veins

As you lie there, sense into your veins and feel your blood pumping through your body. It helps to attune to the thumping of your heartbeat as well. You can then follow that pulse through your arms, legs, and torso. Feel your body pumping and circulating your blood. Imagine seeing the blood move in your veins. What does it feel like to sense this pumping aliveness? What does your blood feel like moving in your body?

Fluids and Organs:
Your Body Is Mostly Made of Water

Place your hands on your belly and locate a felt sense of fluidity within and the organs being supported by those fluids. Sense into the fluids of your body. Your organs are supported by and floating inside these fluids. To feel this a bit more, bend your left knee and place your left foot on the floor. This is your stabilizing foot. With your right leg outstretched, point its toes toward the sky. Begin to rock your right heel forward and back so that it brings some rocking movement all the way through your right leg, into your pelvis, through your torso, and into your whole body. Let your body be heavy, and let the rocking forward and back of your foot ignite a sense of movement that stimulates the fluids in your body. Switch legs when you are ready. Then rest your legs completely and feel the resonance of that gentle fluid wave moving inside you and supporting your organs.

Now come onto your hands and knees in an all-fours position. Feel the weight of your body, and sense into the organs held in your torso. Move gently in any fluid way through your torso, and as you do, bring your awareness to your organs. Sense your organs floating in the fluids of your body as you circulate your spine, shoulders, and hips in this position.

Bones:
Your Body Has a Steady Architecture

Stand with your feet as wide as your hips, your arms by your sides. Feel the weight of your body move down into the bones of your legs. Sense the solidity and density of your bones as you stand right on top of your legs. Now bring your hands to the top rim of your pelvis and push down. Feel the bones of your pelvis and hips connect down into your leg bones, through your ankles, and into your feet. Sense your bones as steady, stable, and creating architecture for your presence. As you continue to push down through the bones of your pelvis and legs with your hands, reach your spine up and out from your pelvis and toward the crown of your head. Get a sense of your vertebrae lengthening. Keeping that tall stance, stretch your arms up to the sky. Straighten your arms to your capacity and feel your bones extending.

You can also sense into the bony structure of your body with a forward fold, bringing your attention to your pelvis settled directly over your legs and feeling the weight move down. Downward-facing dog pose and even a handstand (if those are in your repertoire) are also excellent shapes within which to feel and sense your bones.

Come to rest on your back after these movements. Bend your knees and separate your feet wider than your hips, resting your knees inward on each other. Rest your arms by your sides. With your legs bent in this neutral position for your pelvis, feel the heavy bones of your pelvis and sacrum. Feel the bony angle of your bent knees. Feel the weight of your bony structure completely. Breathe into your bones for a few minutes.

Muscles:
Your Body Has Powerful Tissues

With your feet hip distance apart, squat halfway down to the floor. Hold for ten breaths and feel the muscles of your legs working. Move in and out of this squat several times, each time holding for a few breaths to feel the muscles of your lower body working. Sense the strength of your muscles. Then come into a plank pose, basically the top of a pushup. You can do this with your knees down too if needed. Hold the top of your pushup for five breaths. Feel your arms, legs, and core working to support you. Rest and then repeat a few times. Each time you hold the plank pose, squeeze the muscles of your body and feel into the intensity of the muscular contraction. Rest on your belly after this and let all your muscles soften and relax. Notice the contrast of the muscular engagement you just did in the squats and plank compared with the release of this resting.

A simple but powerful contract-and-release exercise in a chair or on the floor is useful if the preceding exercise does not work for your body or energy, or even if you just want to give this one a try too. Lying on the floor, move sequentially through your body parts, squeezing the muscles as much as possible for a few breaths and then completely letting go. You can follow this sequence: Squeeze the muscles of your feet and ankle for two breaths, and then release for two breaths. Now your lower legs. Then knees. Thighs, then hips. Lowest part of your belly and pelvic floor. Torso and belly. Shoulders, then neck. Upper arms. Lower arms. Then hands by making tense fists. Finally, your face, your scalp, and the back of your skull.

Nervous System:
Your Body Moves Charge

It can be challenging to stay connected to your nervous system unless it is obviously activated, at which point it garners your attention. This movement pattern is intended to help you balance the current of your nervous system. Standing up, begin to hop, jump, and shake a little bit. Feel your heart rate increase. Do this for a minute or two. Then plant your feet underneath you. Continue to shake your body. This movement can be very small. You are creating a vibration of activation in your body with it. Let your body shake for a few more breaths. Pause in stillness and feel the current running through you.

Now come to a kneeling position, sitting on your heels. Sit on a towel or blanket to pad your knees and shins if needed. Place your hands on your thighs and tune in to the currents of your body. Lift up onto your knees and shins as you sweep your arms up overhead. Look up to your hands if that is comfortable for your neck. Then draw your arms in toward your belly as you exhale and sit back on your heels. Repeat this movement pattern a few times. Coordinate your breathing with the movement as best you can. Pay attention to activation, rigidity, electricity, and softness. Sense your system slowing down, integrating, coming back in.

Fat:
Your Body Has Nourishing Insulation

The fat in your body is vital to the nourishment and support of your organs, your brain function, and your nervous system. It is your insulation in a very good way. Think of a wire with no covering. It can short-circuit easily. Fat is this insulation. It nourishes, supports, insulates. Lie down on the floor and rest. Move your attention and awareness into the fat that supports and insulates your body. Feel this layer supporting and nourishing the electrical impulses within your body. Rest into the fat of your body in a way that brings support. Instead of being a live wire, you are a well-nourished and supported organism.

Movement Exercise 2:
Move an Experience or Emotion through Your Body

This is similar to the Show Instead of Tell exercise in that you will use movement to illustrate your experience. Just as you practiced expressing your feelings, or a small event from your day, this exercise invites you to take a narrative from your life— a story from the fabric of your soma—and conjure it through your body. The purpose is not to relive pain or trauma. Quite the contrary, this practice is aimed at helping you weave this narrative more fully into your soma without the need for words and explanations. It is an opportunity to experience and express parts of the story you may not have been able to when it actually occurred. You may find yourself surprised that a new insight, feeling, or quality of memory arises by reworking this story through your body in this way.

You may also choose to work with a particular part or emotion related to the story. For example, perhaps you are ruminating on an argument with your partner that feels unresolved. Take the feeling of irritation or resentment and express it through your body. Maybe what is more important than the argument narrative itself is a chance to reveal and feel what you couldn't in that argument. Maybe there wasn't enough room for your anger to be fully expressed without scaring your partner. So you get a chance to weave that on the loom of your movement consciousness now. You might find that as you do this, other feelings and thoughts that you avoided or pushed down in the actual disagreement have a chance to also be felt and expressed. This is good news. You are intended to feel all of yourself as an active player in your narrative rather than a bystander observing the events.

Choose a story, pattern, or feeling you would like to explore now through your body. Write it down briefly on the lines below. Then place your hands over your heart and bow your head toward your heart as a way to acknowledge this narrative, belief, or feeling and the invitation to explore it through your body.

_____

_____

_____

If you are familiar with and already pretty adept at moving freely in an unchoreographed manner, let yourself move freely with the intention to express this narrative. Stay curious about what new feelings and insights may emerge.

If you have a familiar yoga, dance, or other somatic practice that brings you a safe container within which to move and feel, bring this intention into your practice. Invite this inquiry of story and feeling into your practice. Set the intention to explore and express a particular feeling or experience.

If you are less familiar with moving as a way to express narrative and emotion, here are some movements and postures to try. The first two invitations are inspired by a contemporary somatic practice called The Class, by Taryn Toomey.

1. Stand with your feet a bit wider than your hips, and bend your knees. Shift your weight from side to side and front to back. You can place your hands on your body to help connect yourself more. Once you have felt your weight shift a bit, begin to lift your heels up off the floor and then drop them back down. This will help you to simply arrive in your body. As you tap your heels onto the floor with the rhythm of your breathing, conjure the narrative or feeling you wish to explore. Name it to yourself. Notice any impulses that arise. Perhaps you want to immediately freeze and stop moving. Perhaps you want to swing your arms. Perhaps you want to move more vigorously. Perhaps you want to reach your arms up over

your head or fold forward over your legs. Let yourself do this! May this be a springboard for some movement.

2. Stand in a wide squat with your feet turned out. Bend your knees. Place your hands on your body and connect to your breath as well as the story, feeling, or belief you intend to explore. Pulse up and down in your legs, creating some movement. Let your arms hang free. Use the pulsing action of the squat to assist you in evoking the story lines or heart threads. Let your arms and upper body move freely. If you feel your body's impulse to move in another way, let yourself do this. See what happens and how you want to move with this as a starting point.

3. Start in a simple child's pose, with your toes touching, your knees open wider than your waist, your torso bowed to the ground, and your arms stretched forward or by your sides. Feel the weight of your body and the movement of your breath. Set your intention here to evoke, express, and feel what needs to be explored. Come up to your hands and knees, on all fours. Begin to move in any manner that feels good to you: rocking your weight forward and back on your hands and knees; rounding and extending your spine; wagging your hips and circulating in your shoulders. Let this fluid movement spur some further free movement for you. Maybe you'll find your way down onto your back and onto the floor. Or maybe you'll find yourself crawling, or finding a way to stand.

Journal Inquiry:
Stories Living in Your Body

Of course, feel free to reflect on any of the movement practices you have explored earlier. In addition, you can go through these prompts. Spend a few minutes considering what stories live in your body. There may be some obvious ones, such as giving birth to your child, being in a car accident, being assaulted, playing a sport continuously, experiencing a graduation or rite of passage. There may be ones that go less noticed, like moving to a new house or accepting a job offer. There may even be ones that are encoded within you but you do not remember, such as your time in your mother's womb, your own birth, or the impact of your parents' separation or reunion.

1. List the most obvious events that you know have impacted your body or that you can tell live inside your body. Where in your body do you feel these stories are held? What lives in your bones? What lives in your spine? What experiences live in your uterus? What story might be longing to be told from your throat? Also write down what sensations arise in your body as you write the experience down. With all of this, do not overthink. Simply write down what surfaces and what you feel.

_____

_____

_____

_____

2. List the events and experiences of which you have a less clear picture of in your memory but that you sense live in the fabric of your soma. Consider events that may be unprocessed—whose texture is still very present in your skin but have not been rewoven into the whole tapestry. You may be able to tell that something is undigested because you repeatedly have sensations in a part of your body and do not necessarily know why. Is there a feeling or pattern of sensations that turn up in a part of your body and you lack words or memory or a clear understanding of why?

_____

_____

_____

_____

3. List any sensations, patterns of movement, or chronic somatic symptoms you experience that could potentially be pointing you toward larger feelings, memories, and stories. Tune in to the different systems of your body as best you can, and ask what energy or stories may be held there. Again, pay attention to sensations that emerge as you write these down.

_____

_____

_____

_____

Creative Exercise:
Image the Stories of Your Body

This is a creative project I learned from one of my mentors, Melissa Michaels, in her seminal program Surfing the Creative. I have used iterations of it with students and clients over the years as well as in my own process. I share it with you as a way to visualize and externalize the stories living in the fabric of your soma. Trust yourself as you put image to paper to express and externalize visually these deeply woven threads.

To create this body drawing, you will need some large sheets of paper and whatever paints, magazines, pastels, or crayons you like to use to express yourself. First, you will need to create a tracing of your body. You can make a life-size tracing by lying down on a large enough piece of paper and having someone trace the outline of your body. You can also do a tracing of your own hands or your feet. This is often a good option if you do not have someone to trace your whole body, if you do not have a large enough paper, or if it simply feels daunting to undertake your whole body! You can trace the outline of your hands or feet on any large enough piece of paper using a pen or crayon.

Once you have the tracing, fill it in with images from magazines, cards, paper, and so forth. You can use paints to create images or shapes as well. Don't be afraid to mix media forms as you express the stories that live inside your body. Consider what stories live inside you. Use some of your journaling as a guide.

Real-Life Engagement:
Slow Down to Embody before Mentalizing

Whether we like it or not, we experience life through our bodies. And yet it is typical to move into analysis and thinking before really dropping into feeling and being with what is present in our bodies. Our culture often prioritizes thinking over feeling, analyzing and creating meaning over being present and marinating ourselves in the moment. Despite the belief that thinking things through is an efficient way to process experiences, this mentalizing actually takes us out of our embodied experience.

Slowing down, taking time to feel the impact of what is happening or what has been said, and staying present in your body actually takes you right into the waves of life. It makes you more vulnerable, yes. But it is also more efficient and is the direct and active weaving process of your soma. This exercise primes you to slow down enough to be present with what is happening before trying to figure it out or analyze it with your mind. If you have a strong coping strategy of mentalizing or analyzing before feeling, this practice will take some time. Like most things that are not innate, this is a practice.

It goes like this: When you are having a conversation with someone, commit to allowing yourself to feel the impact of their words. If you are eating, invite yourself into the full experience of eating—the smells, the tastes, the company. If you are in a disagreement with your partner, challenge yourself to feel the fullness of your frustration while staying connected to the felt sense of your core, the back of your body, and your feet. If you find yourself popping up into your mind to analyze what is happening, soften your knees and lean back into your spine. Take a slow breath. Notice how you feel in the presence of this moment. Commit to this process of slowing down and then feeling into your body before analyzing, answering, or figuring things out.

CHAPTER 8

Your Body Has Innate Pathways for Healing

I had a miscarriage when I was thirty-five. The event and experience of it was largely straightforward and involved few complications. From the outside, I was healthy and recovered well. Even psychologically I felt at peace with the situation as it was—resolved. Some months later, I began to feel unrest. A kind of unnamable grief and anger arose in waves. My heart felt heavy and sad, welling with energy that I could tell needed to move. Intense sensations including a strong tightness, burning, and scraping would swirl in my lower abdomen. As someone with a steady movement practice, I took these feelings into my dance and yoga spaces. I moved the energy living in this part of my body, as well as all the tiny bits of unresolved pain and loss. There were still places that needed to be processed, parts of the story that needed to be released from the tissues, places that needed to be rewoven from having been frayed in this biologically normal, but nonetheless difficult and extreme, experience. I shook my body vigorously, stomped, flushed, and flapped my arms. I made gestures to move any energy further stuck in my organs and uterus. I vocalized the story of this loss, including its hurt, confusion, grief, and relief, through my throat and my bones, not in words, just in sounds. I cried and held myself in dignity and compassion—the kind of crying that lands you on a new shore. There were not many words or explanations to be had. I moved until the energy was complete. I came to a new doorway of peace. I felt settled. I could feel the story resting differently. I was more whole again.

~

Your psyche, your heart, and your body know at a deep level how to reorient toward a flow of health and vitality. Regardless of how far away from that you may feel, there is some pulse within you that can continually find a way to process, locate health, and find homeostasis. Edward Podvoll wrote in *Recovering Sanity* that we each have an "island of sanity" within us that remains untouched and unscathed by the various torrents of neuroses or extreme states of mind we might experience.[63] When we have encountered trauma, suffer in cycles of addiction or chronic pain, find ourselves anxious or depressed, or loop in destructive thoughts, too often we think that we are defective. We think that something about us must be "off" or incapable, that we are the problem, that we need experts to fix and heal us. We can get miles away from our center and from trusting our innate intelligence within.

Of course, there are times when medication for chronic mind states and support from professionals in unwinding trauma and wounding are vital and necessary to restoring health, sanity, and functionality to our systems. Somatic work can help return your system to a state of balance in which this healing and restoring intelligence is not impeded. Somatic therapies restore the balance of your somatic intelligence—that embodied capacity you were born with—which knows how to find its way. When this river flows freely, it's not that you do not get sick or hurt or have difficulty. Rather, you are able to find your way through and back toward health more readily and easily. Gabrielle Roth wrote in *Maps to Ecstasy*, "Put the psyche in motion and it will heal itself."[64] Her work encourages us to take our bodies and our whole selves through waves of movement to restore balance, harmony, and sanity in our systems. Along the way, we may visit deeply uncomfortable, insightful material and vivid sensations. The result that follows is a sense of deep peace. Ida Rolf, creator of the bodywork practice known as Rolfing Structural Integration, offered the notion that the human body has a somatic architectural blueprint imprinting and coordinating our structure and movement.[65] If we are far from this optimal architectural framework, we feel pain, have structural and muscular imbalances, and are more likely to experience injury.[66] Supporting the fascial alignment of the body allows one's bones and muscles access to a more unencumbered sense of mobility, which often translates to emotional and psychological benefit.[67]

Your body has innate intelligence to support, express, and heal itself. When a bone breaks, it grows bone tissue to knit the broken parts back together. When you exercise and put strain on your muscles, little tears in the muscle fibers occur and then reweave themselves to be stronger to that pressure than before. When you get a cut, your immune system kicks in to prevent infection and your skin heals itself by scabbing over and growing again. Laboring mothers show us the power of the human body to orient in and through difficult and even extreme processes that literally birth new life. Healing and repair are innate to our bodies' capacity. Somatic psychology and related therapies take the premise that this cellular healing intelligence permeates other areas of the human organism—in our psyches and emotions.[68]

Movement practices can be used as an intervention for physical, psychological, and emotional needs. Often, the intervention chosen ultimately impacts all these layers of our being. Somatic therapies utilize movement patterns and sequences to integrate our life experiences, release stress and overwhelm, and unwind and mitigate trauma. Of course, this then impacts our movement repertoires by restoring capacities that may have previously been interrupted or truncated. When we are given the opportunity to find a true and authentic "No" and express it physically through gesture or pushing away, this restored boundary brings about a renewed physical freedom. When we are able to finally feel an authentic desire well up inside us and find a healthy way of expressing itself physically, life force and power are reignited.

Somatic approaches also utilize movement exercises to support physical imbalances, rewire motor impairments, and facilitate physical healing. This of course can have a direct impact on one's psychological and emotional imprints. If you have ever had chronic pain due to a physical injury or imbalance, you know how taxing this state can be. Being in pain continuously takes an immense amount of energy. It is stressful and consuming. If a somatic intervention can support one's body to find a reduction in or freedom from pain, not only does the injury itself begin to heal fully, but the energy it took to withstand such pain is freed up. Somatic therapies value this truth:

Your body has innate pathways for healing.

Sequencing

Sequencing is a concept that illustrates your body's capacity to unwind itself from tension, dis-ease, and trauma to return to satisfying homeostatic balance. It illustrates your body's capacity to orient and move energy in waves. *Sequencing* is the process of identifying a movement impulse or pattern that needs a fuller expression to come all the way to completion.[69] In this practice, you may notice a sensation or feeling that seems tense or unresolved. You may notice a movement pattern in your body that needs some room to breathe and free itself up. It takes a lot of energy and life force to hold emotions and movement impulses back. Allow the energy of your body-mind to move freely, tracking its flow.

Healthy Tone

Healthy tone denotes the state of one's neurological activity in muscular balance. Rather than muscular activity being overactive in a hypertonic state, or underengaged in a hypotonic state, healthy tone brings one into presence and functionality without collapse or rigidity. Muscular tone links to other areas of one's capacity as well. Quality of muscular tone is often linked to nervous system activation and other neurological patterns.[70] It can denote a passive response system or one that is in hyperdrive. For example, when a person is in a state of hyperalertness and their nervous system is stuck in sympathetic arousal, we see a corresponding physiological hypervigilance in their muscular tone. People who live in a chronic state of such hyperarousal can experience chronic muscular tension, fatigue, clenching, and overreactivity. On the other end of the spectrum, we see hypotonic muscular activity linked to hyporeactivity in the nervous system.[71] A lethargic, flaccid, underengaged musculature and responsiveness are displayed in this chronic state. Learning to track this pattern and finding ways to return to healthy tone in the muscular engagement links to the capacity to restore healthy activity in the nervous system, the ability to rise and fall through states of arousal and back into rest. Making it a practice to continually reorient to healthy, relaxed, but present states of alertness and engagement in which you are neither gripping nor collapsing can be healing unto itself. Not only does it help your body find more ease in its engagement capacity, but it also helps your nervous system restore balance. This also translates to the ways in which you commune with the world and relationships around you as you learn to find a healthy tone for your whole soma.

Movement Exercise:
Sequencing

Use the following three movement exercises to experiment with sequencing your own soma. Trust your innate capacity to follow your instincts and your body's knowing toward satisfying waves of emotional, physical, and psychological release and reorientation.

Move discomfort or pain. If you feel pain or discomfort in your body and you are constantly poking or prodding or fidgeting to find some relief, try pausing, taking a full breath with your eyes closed, and placing your hands on your body where you feel the pain. Bring your presence, loving contact, and breath to where it hurts. Engage the principle that your body can find a healthy path to move out of pain and tension. Let your sensations be the guide here. Wiggle, expand or contract, and sway as you follow the pathway of discomfort through and out of your body. This may not resolve what is going on completely, but it can provide some relief and guidance. If an emotion arises as you do this, do not hold back. Let the tears come. Since emotions are embedded somatically, as you free up the flow of energy and movement in your body, you also thaw the river of emotion.

Rest into the part of you that knows. Lean against a support at your back: a wall or a tree or some stacked pillows, something that you can lean back into and practice yielding and softening into the back of your body. Close your eyes or soften your gaze. Bring the sense of your front body all the way toward your back body. Give the full weight of your body to the supports behind you. This resting drains excess tension from your body and enlivens any overwhelming fatigue.

Sequence an emotion. We can learn to ride waves of emotions as they well up, swell and crest, crash onto the shores of our consciousness, and recede out into peace again. Sometimes our emotional states need encouragement and guidance to move all the way through our systems to completion. No emotion is better or worse than another. All are true and equally innate to our humanness. Of course, there will be tendencies within each of us to feel some emotions more frequently, easily, and intensely than others. No emotion is intended to be felt forever. They are temporary experiences, albeit deep and consuming in the moment. Use this practice to help you build the capacity to ride waves of emotions.

Tune in and notice whether there is an emotion that needs some space to move. Perhaps you have been gripping around fear or grief. Perhaps you have not let your joy rush in like sun streaming through the windows. Perhaps anger must well like a fire and purge through and out of you. If you feel an emotion welling up and you have the capacity to move with it sans much guidance, please by all means use your practices to follow its expression here. The postures that follow may help if you need some support in doing so.

For truncated anger that needs to move, try pushing against a wall as hard as you can. As you push your arms into the wall, push down through your legs too. Let your face and voice express. If from this you have the urge to move in another way, let yourself. Stay connected to your feet and your breath the entire time.

For grief that needs some space, try standing up with your legs a bit wider than your hips. Breathe your arms up over your head and, with a big sigh, swiftly release your arms and torso down in a forward bend. Repeat this a few times. Breathe in and up; then throw your arms and torso down with a big exhale. Soften into a forward bend. Find a gentle bend in your knees. Clasp your hands to opposite elbows and let your torso swing a little. Soften your face, jaw, and tongue, and release any sighs as you gently sway.

For fear that needs to ground, shake your body. As you shake your body, imagine all the fear you feel draining out of you as if you are draining a bathtub. Sense and internally watch this fear drain from your cells. Once you have done this for a few moments, pause and feel the vibration as you solidify your sense of weight in your feet and into the ground. Use this connection to bring you a sense of support and safe ground upon which to stand. Breathe this up your legs and into your belly.

Journal Inquiry:
Gather Insights

Use the prompts below to help you reflect, gathering some embodied wisdom after your movement experiment. Add other notes to yourself and insights as you have them.

THE DIFFERENCE IN MY BODY BETWEEN HOLDING ENERGY I FEEL INSIDE AND LETTING IT MOVE COMPLETELY THROUGH AND OUT OF MY BODY IS ...

THIS IS WHAT I NOTICED WHEN I SEQUENCED THE ENERGY/EMOTION OF _____ THROUGH MY BODY.

OTHER REFLECTIONS:

Creative Exercise:
Sequence on Paper

Identify a place inside your body, an emotion, or an experience that feels a little unfinished or incomplete. Choose something that you would like to externalize onto paper and see reflected back to you. With pastels or watercolors (or whatever you have), take the unfinished business of the energy, feeling, or story, and paint or draw it out. Don't worry about being a "good" artist. Simply allow the energy to move onto the page through colors, gestures, and shapes. Notice what it feels like to channel this less digested energy into a creative project. Notice if you feel a bit more resolved or complete in having externalized this energy or feeling.

Real-Life Engagement:
Practice Orienting to Health

This might sound rather obvious, but your practice in everyday life is to continually orient toward what is life-affirming and healthy. Practice letting yourself find pathways of support, nourishment, satisfaction, and wholeness. There are many ways to maintain and live from this place of deep knowing and trust that your body and psyche can support its own healing. I encourage you to think of your own ways to practice this out in the world, but here are a few.

Release Your Day. Make ending your day a small ritual. Thank it and your showing up in it. Release it and put it to bed. Shower and let the energy of the day fall off you like the water does. Let the day drain. Make a conscious effort to release the day and all of its happenings. Feel yourself being and breathing regardless of how well the day went or how much you accomplished.

Clear Boundaries. Set boundaries that keep you in relationship with yourself and others. You have already garnered a sense of healthy boundaries—what they are, how to identify them, and how to set them. Making clear boundaries over and over again that communicate your heart and your capacity will help to give your soma riverbanks of safety and movement.

Release and Channel Excess Energy. Remember that your body stores information not just in the form of story and narrative but also in emotions and energy. It is vital that these have places to move through you. The more you give room for the energy in your body and feelings to move, the more natural it is for your soma to stay connected to its intuitive flow. If you feel a lot of frustration or tension, an emotion that simply won't budge, shake your body to release some of that energy. As you engage in this rhythm of shaking and release, consciously encourage the energy and emotion to move through your body.

Find Healthy Tone. In every aspect of your day—every activity and conversation— orient to healthy tone. Track when, where, and with whom you become rigid or collapsed. As you notice this hypo or hyper tone, breathe and reorient to a healthy, present balance. Locate the felt sense of balanced tone whenever and wherever you can.

PART 3

Journey through the Soma

CHAPTER 9

Cultivate Ongoing Embodiment

As a culture, I find we are desperate to return to our embodiment. We are desperate for practices that will help us be truly ourselves; we long for containers of expression in which we can actually feel ourselves and what is true and emergent in the moment without fear of judgment, ridicule, mistake, or injury. Having a basket of embodiment practices that you can choose from daily can help nourish and cultivate balance, always moving you into the direct experience of your soma.

Movement is in dynamic relationship with both your unconscious mind[72] and your nervous system.[73] Movement has the capacity to regulate, support, and soothe places of activation, stress, and overwhelm in your body. Embodiment and movement practices take you directly into the felt experience of your body to meet your nervous system responses exactly where they are in each moment.[74] Movement also has the capacity to stir the pot, to bring unconscious material to the surface.[75] It has the ability to thaw what has long been frozen. Body-mind connection is a bidirectional somatic highway: Movement to evoke. Movement to contain. Movement to discover. Movement to recover. Movement to express. Movement to digest.

Of course, moving one's body does not necessarily translate to embodiment. It is possible to move and be totally disconnected from the experience of moving. Furthermore, embodiment is not entirely dependent on obvious outer movement. It is possible to be quite limited in range of motion for any number of reasons and still have the capacity to track inward movement of the soma, thus yielding embodiment. Healthy embodiment practices yoke your movement to your inner awareness. If you already have a steady movement practice, incorporate these practices into them. Perhaps you have a routine of going to the gym or running or hiking. You can infuse these activities with a presence of embodiment and somatic awareness within all movements and activities. If you feel a dearth of movement opportunities, establishing a routine practice within which to deepen your embodiment safely is just as important as any other health and wellness habit, routine, or goal you might cultivate. If you have specific limitations and needs regarding your mobility, you can incorporate sensory awareness tracking throughout your body even while lying down, seated, or supported by another individual.

Grounding

Grounding is using your inner insight—sensing and feeling—to connect your body and energy into the earth.[76] Getting grounded invites you to pause and pay attention to the ever-present support of the earth beneath your feet, to connect to the source of steadiness beneath you even when things may feel shaky or chaotic. It can be done barefoot on the sand or grass, sitting on a rock, lying on the earth, sitting in a chair, or lying on the floor of your apartment. Grounding is a useful tool no matter where or who you are, what you are doing, or who you are with.

Real-Life Engagement:
Practice Getting Grounded

Take a few minutes right now to ground with and through your body and breath. Preferably, find a place outside for this practice to be on the earth—be it on a rock, on grass, on sand or moss, or against a tree. If that is not an option, use what you have. Connect with a ground that feels supportive and organic enough.

Take off your shoes and socks. Stand steady in your feet and feel them connect to the ground or floor beneath you. You can wiggle your toes a bit and oscillate your balance across your feet with a soft bend in your knees. Draw your attention to the bottoms of your feet and the sensation of your feet touching the earth or the floor. Connect down, as far down as you can, into the earth and imagine yourself rooting there just as any root system of a tree would do. Notice your breathing, and consciously soften and deepen your breath as you continue to root down. Next, draw this energy of the earth up through your feet and your legs, through your belly and chest, and into your neck and head, letting it stream down your arms and into your fingers. Feel your whole being connecting to the earth. Breathe deeply. Let any sighs happen. Stay soft. Connect. Notice what a few minutes of grounding your energy in this way does for your system. This practice is right here, available to you day or night.

Reflections

WHEN I AM GROUNDED, I FEEL ...

THIS IS ME WHEN I AM GROUNDED AND CONNECTED:

_____ HELPS ME GET GROUNDED.

Breath and Movement

We are generally programmed to move through our daily lives without much attention to this miracle that is the act of breathing in a body. If you are breathing, you are alive. Your heart is beating and pumping blood just like every other human being on the earth. This breath courses in and out of your lungs, supporting your functioning and living, until the day is done. One of the most awakening and nourishing components of a healthy embodied practice is the way it marries moving and breathing. Many activities tend toward a pattern of moving *and then* paying attention to any breathing changes. Embodied movement practices invite you to move *while* you are aware of your breathing, moving from your breathing patterns, and even linking breath patterns with movements.

Below are two simple practices for you to try and even pair together. The first is a simple breathing exercise, and the second is a practice of linking your breath with movement.

Movement Exercise:
Practice Simple Breathing

Find a comfortable place to sit or lie down. Settle into your seat, or the floor, or your bed, and close your eyes. Spend five rounds of breath simply becoming more aware that you are being breathed. Move your consciousness close to the rhythm and functioning of your breathing. Over the next five breaths, pay attention to what moves—what rises and falls as you breathe. Does your belly move in and out the most? Are your ribs the most mobile? Is the top of your chest moving the most when you breathe?

Place your hands on the part of your torso that has the greatest ease of movement when you breathe. As you consciously deepen your breaths, send some energy and aliveness from this most free place into the spaces of your torso that may feel a bit more sticky, contracted, or frozen. Notice what happens. For some, sending the resource of one's freer breath into the more contracted places begins to loosen up the sticky spots. For others, it becomes fairly obvious almost immediately which parts of one's being are most contracted.

Next, begin to expand your breath as best you can in each direction. Breathe into the front and back of your body. (If you are leaning on a chair or wall or lying on a bed, feel the back of your body move into that support.) Notice what it feels like to breathe fully and deeply into the front and back of you.

Now breathe lengthwise from the very bottom of your pelvic floor all the way to the top of your chest. Move your breath from top to bottom, creating length here. All the way up. All the way down.

Next, breathe as much as you can into the width of your torso. Feel your ribs expanding, feel the sides of your body expanding, and allow your inhale to really push the boundary of your sides, feeling the exhale draw your ribs down and your waist inward.

Finally, take a few rounds of breath to breathe fully circumferentially throughout your entire torso. Let your breathing be a full experience inside.

Reflections

WHERE DID IT FEEL PARTICULARLY STICKY OR DIFFICULT TO BREATHE FULLY?

WHERE DID IT FEEL EASY TO BREATHE MOST FULLY?

BREATHING CIRCUMFERENTIALLY IN ALL DIRECTIONS FEELS ...

_____

_____

_____

WHEN MY BREATH IS STUCK, I FEEL ...

_____

_____

WHEN MY BREATH IS FULL, I FEEL ...

_____

_____

_____

Movement Exercise:
Practice Linking Breath with Movement

Stand comfortably and softly, with a gentle bend in your knees. When you inhale, draw your arms up by your sides in big arcs until your hands touch overhead. Pause at the top and stretch up. On your exhale, lower your arms down the same way. Repeat this for about a minute: reaching your arms up as you inhale, pausing, exhaling as you lower your arms down. Subtly and slowly shift your awareness to originate this movement from your breath. Your arms lift because your inhale lifts them. Your arms move back down because your exhale moves them.

Use this very basic movement as a base upon which to add other breath-based movements. You can explore twisting from one side to the next, linking your breath to motivate this movement. You can add a simple forward fold, again having the breath really lead the way of the movement. For those of you already familiar with yoga postural practice, you know that the sun salutations are wonderful expressions of moving from your breath. Play with having all your movement emanate from and be inspired by your breath, truly moving from the inside out.

Reflections

WHEN I MOVE FROM MY BREATH, I NOTICE ...

THIS IS WHAT MOVING FROM BREATHING FEELS LIKE:

THE DIFFERENCE FOR ME BETWEEN MOVING, THEN BREATHING, AND BREATHING TO MOVE IS ...

Moving through Endpoints

Your endpoints are the parts of you that make contact with the world around you. These points of giving to and receiving from your world are your toes and feet, your fingers and hands, the top of your head, and your tailbone.[77] The mouth and face are often considered to be another endpoint, as they are critical for gesture and communication. From a somatic therapy perspective, when we are encouraging full embodiment, we are encouraging energy and aliveness to inhabit fully through the whole soma, including these endpoints.[78]

One of the quickest ways I have found to draw yoga students into their bodies more deeply, and to encourage their embodied experience, is to invite them into awareness of their endpoints. It's as if suddenly there is more presence in their bodies. Suddenly they are moving to and from the edges of their being. When we dare to inhabit our bodies fully, up to the very edges, we allow ourselves to take up more space, to live at the shores of our developmental edges of movement, emotion, and sensing, and to be fully engaged. I encourage you to try these exercises to enliven your embodiment too. Let the extension of your aliveness move all the way from your insides out through your limbs and into your endpoints. Allow these points of contact to receive the world around you and draw it into yourself.

Movement Exercise:
Practice Exploring Your Endpoints

Lie on your back, stretching your arms and legs out and open as you inhale. Stretch all the way from the core of your body through your arms and legs, feet and hands, tailbone and crown. You can even stretch the muscles of your face. As you exhale, curl into a ball. Draw your navel to your spine and your limbs into your belly, rounding your head toward your knees. Repeat this movement a few times, moving in and out from your core to your endpoints.

Standing up, step your feet wide. Stretch your arms wide and slightly up toward the sky, as if you were a five-pointed star. Reach down into your feet and toes, down through your tailbone, out through your arms and hands, and upward through your neck and into the crown of your head. Feel energy circulate from your endpoints to your spine and back out. Contrast this by standing in a relaxed way with your legs right under you and your arms by your sides. Find presence and awareness through your endpoints even in this relaxed stance.

Reflections

Consider that your endpoints are the points at which you give and receive contact with the world around you.

BRINGING MY ATTENTION TO MY ENDPOINTS FEELS ...

_____

_____

_____

THESE ENDPOINTS FELT AWAKE:

_____

_____

_____

THESE ENDPOINTS FELT DULL:

_____

_____

Moving with Rhythm

Experimenting with different rhythms through our bodies opens our capacity for wider movements, lessens self-consciousness that sometimes accompanies being in a body, and reestablishes our innate capacity to feel and respond to life's ever-evolving, emergent, and changing rhythms.[79] Swaying or rocking, pushing or jumping, shaking, and stillness are some of the most basic movement rhythms of our lives.

Below are exercises to encourage your exploration of rhythm in your body. Being and moving in various rhythms assists embodiment. You can do these exercises below individually or in the order given. If you choose the latter, notice what it feels like to move through all of them in a sequence. There is medicine in linking them together sequentially for a full embodiment repertoire exercise. There is also medicine in choosing one to support your energy right now.

Movement Exercise:
Practice Moving in Rhythm

Rocking or swaying. Bring a gentle swaying or rocking into your body. Stand with a soft bend in your knees. Hold a soft gaze in your eyes. Begin to sway or rock back and forth gently. Keep your neck and head soft, even bowing your head slightly toward your heart. You can also do this sitting in a chair. Let yourself be soothed, nourished, and supported by this rhythm. Notice what it feels like to move in this way. Pay attention to resistance too.

Reflections

ROCKING FEELS TO ME LIKE ...

_____

_____

_____

SWAYING HELPS ME FEEL ...

_____

_____

_____

WHEN I ROCK OR SWAY, I REMEMBER OR AM REMINDED OF ...

_____

_____

_____

I NOTICE _____ WHEN I AM IN THIS RHYTHM.

_____

_____

Pushing or jumping. Come to a wall and place your hands on the wall with your feet slightly staggered for balance, one a bit behind the other. With your arms, push the wall. As you do this, imagine pushing from your core through your arms and into the wall. As you push into the wall, feel strength pressing down through your legs. Tears, frustration, and sound of any kind are all fair game as you connect to your capacity to push with your arms. Push more with one arm, then with the other, and notice the difference between the sides.

Now explore pushing through your lower body by jumping. Stand with your feet hip-width apart, and bend your knees toward a squat. Jump up and land again in the same spot. Do this a few times. Pay particular attention to the push down through your legs—from your core into your legs and feet into the floor.

Reflections

WHEN I PUSH THROUGH MY ARMS, I FEEL ...

_____

_____

_____

WHEN I PUSH DOWN THROUGH MY LEGS, I FEEL ...

_____

_____

_____

THE SENSE OF PUSHING HELPS ME ...

_____

_____

_____

Shaking. Simply put, shake your body. Or, offered another way, let your body shake. Begin by shaking each arm and hand, then each leg and foot. Shake your hips and then your shoulders. Fold over slightly, loosen your jaw and the muscles of your face, and gently shake your head. When you feel comfortable enough to do so, move your whole body in this shaking rhythm. If a sound arises, let it come and move through you too. Stay curious and trust the process of letting yourself shake. If something comes up that you want to shake off or out, please do. Explore what this rhythm does for you: it helps you clear out, helps you soften into.

Reflections

SHAKING FEELS LIKE ...

_____

_____

_____

_____ COMES UP FOR ME WHEN I LET MYSELF SHAKE.

_____

_____

Stillness. Kneel on the floor or sit with your back against a wall or in a chair. Sit with ease. Close your eyes. Place your hands somewhere on your body. (I like placing one hand on my belly and one hand over my heart the best.) Breathe consciously. Let your heart rate slow down as you feel your heart beating. Imagine the blood being pumped through your veins. Sit in stillness and quiet. No rigidity or collapse here. Practice quiet and still presence.

Reflections

WHEN I AM CONSCIOUSLY STILL, I AM ...

_____

_____

IN STILLNESS I CAN FEEL ...

_____

_____

_____

_____

_____

Moving from Sensate Awareness

Moving from your capacity to feel and stay connected to the sensations in your body builds your capacity to move from within, to move from what moves you, to move from what is truly yours, to move spontaneously, and to move authentically from impulses and innate desires.[80] It is the basis upon which we can receive information about our inner experience as we move. Moving this way builds a kind of inner trust in which we rely on the organicity of our system and body to move in ever-nourishing ways. You explored this in the previous section, and it is an excellent practice to return to. You will find this practice applicable to other movement practices you may already have. For example, if you have a steady yoga practice, begin exploring how you can be inside a posture and, rather than adjusting yourself within that shape from an intellectual place of "right" alignment, finding a way to self-organize based on the sensations you feel.

Movement Exercise:
Practice Shifting Posture from Sensation

Sit cross-legged on the floor, or sit on a chair with your feet on the floor. Sit tall in your spine and feel breath move in all directions throughout your torso. Feel for a groundedness in your pelvis connecting you to the floor or chair.

Close your eyes or soften your gaze out in front of you so your awareness is turned inward as much as possible. Connect to the inner sensations of your body. If at any time you get flooded or feel blank inside, simply place your hands on your body and connect to the feeling of your hands on your skin. Feel the outline of your skin.

From here, identify a sensation in your body. Give the sensation a "voice" by moving from it. The movement originating from the sensation can be big or small, fast or slow. Stay curious as you let the sensation you feel guide and inspire the movements of your body.

Repeat this process, beginning in the following postures and shapes:

- **Five Pointed Star.** Standing with your feet wide apart and arms stretching out to your sides

- **Mountain Pose.** Standing with feet hip distance apart and your arms stretching up

- **Wide Leg Sit.** Seated with your legs stretched wide apart

- **Child's Pose.** Bowing toward the floor with your big toes touching, knees wider than your torso, forehead on the floor (or a pillow for support), and arms either comfortable by your sides or stretched out in front of you

- **Lunge Pose.** Standing with one leg in front of you bent at the knee and the other leg straight behind you. Stretching your arms up overhead.

Reflections

FOLLOWING THE SENSATIONS IN MY BODY THROUGH MOVEMENT HELPS ME TO ...

_____

_____

_____

_____

WHEN I WAS IN THE _____ SHAPE, I NOTICED _____ AND THEN FOUND MYSELF MOVING LIKE _____.

_____

_____

_____

_____

_____

_____

_____

Moving Organically

Your body is not designed solely for routinized and repetitive movements such as running, biking, or executing a golf swing. We are, however, meant to move in a full spectrum. Your ability to move freely in your body, through all planes of movement, is your birthright. Embodiment practices invite organic movements and expressions—movements that flow through you because they are authentic representations of how you are moved by a song, or by life, or by the current of emotion within you. Expanding this capacity for movement possibility is healthy not only for releasing places in your movement spectrum that have become crystallized and stuck like a broken record, but also for opening up your capacity to feel more fully and freely. One of the greatest gifts of embodied movement practices is its capacity to move us out of self-consciousness and into consciousness of self, where we are fully present, awake, and enlivened within our own skin and far less concerned, if at all, with the judgments or perceptions of others as we live fully in our bodies.[81]

Movement Exercise:
Practice Free-Form Movement

Put on two songs that you love. Dance to them. Literally move however you want to these tracks. If you feel inspired to dance longer, do that! If not, phew, get through two songs, moving in any way that feels good. Then rest a few moments. If your children are around, great! Involve them in this play. Let everyone enjoy moving in their own unique way. No right or wrong, only curiosity. Pay attention to where you feel self-conscious or stiff or silly or weird. Notice where you feel free.

You can expand this practice into a longer format. Choose five different songs that have different melodies, rhythms, and cadences. Choose different genres and lyrics as well. Move freely to them as you choose. Explore how your body moves differently to different rhythms and beats. Explore essentially what turns you on and what lands dull for you. If you begin to feel spacey or ungrounded in your dancing, return to your breathing practices and your grounding.

Reflections

MOVING FREELY IN MY BODY FEELS ...

WHEN I TRY TO MOVE FREELY IN MY BODY, I ...

TODAY, THESE ARE THE INSIGHTS I HAVE GATHERED FROM MY MOVEMENT:

CHAPTER 10

Cultivate Resources

As a therapist, I work with clients through resourcing predominantly as a way to help them navigate symptoms of trauma, which include various states of systemic overload or what we call activation. These symptoms can be rapid eye movements and the inability to make eye contact, fidgeting, fatigue, anxiety, hopelessness, or despair, just to name a few. Resources in this way allow them to reorient toward their embodiment in the moment and ride the waves of emotions in their process of healing.[82] Working through trauma is not the only place in which resourcing is helpful, though. I find that identifying and leaning into our resources supports overall well-being. Often we do not even realize how much we have been holding, how tightly we have been wound, or the overwhelm we live with daily. In our culture, *doing* often replaces the simplicity and inherent value of *being*. Resources are ways in which we find refuge, relief, and sustainable balance from feeling stressed, overwhelmed, overstimulated, or activated. Practicing them strengthens our gratitude muscle, increases our capacity to ride intensity in daily life, and heightens our awareness toward peace and joy, even in the face of challenge, difficulty, or grief.

Some of my most exquisite internal experiences have been when I am both well-resourced and in a deep emotional process. It feels as if I can be with all that is not okay in a way that is poignant and filled with beauty—not devoid of pain, of course, but also filled with compassion, capacity, and presence. When I am both resourced and in process, I feel alive and embodied. I am supported in actively working through my emotions rather than being taken by them. In this way, resourcing supports resilience. Resources also fill our cup when we are depleted; they help us return to generativity. Consider that your embodiment and presence are your most precious resources of relating. It needs to be tended to and renewed, and in so doing, is the nourishment that supports your journey of healing—even from trauma that has torn you or your life apart.

Resources do three things: *slow, lower, and contain*. They slow your experience down to a pace that is manageable. They lower the intensity of your experience so it is digestible. They contain your experience, enabling you stay in your body. *Internal resources* are brilliant at balancing a tendency toward being too far outside yourself and engaged in the world. If you feel overwhelmed and outside yourself, bring yourself home with some internal resourcing. *External resources* can support you in coming out of your shell of stuckness. If you feel too far drawn into yourself, if you experience flooding of internal sensations, or if you feel as if you might jump out of your skin, then supporting yourself by connecting with the outer world can help. Resourcing is a practice of tending to your nervous system so you can continue to inhabit your body and your life as fully as possible.

Make resourcing yourself a powerful practice of embodiment. Learning to utilize resources in challenging situations will aid in your resilience capacity. The practice of nourishing through refilling your resources may even help you dismantle what I call the self-care industrial complex—self-care that has become hypertrendy and commodified through crystals, oils, spas, and the push to vacate our lives as if care of self were something to be purchased rather than continuously generated internally.

Internal Resources

Internal resources are the resources you can lean into internally. They are generated from within, always present as a wellspring for our reorientation. Take a look at this list of internal resources. As you go through the list, pause and practice each one for a moment or two. See what resonates with you. Highlight or put an asterisk by the ones that feel most powerful to you. There is a bit of space below each internal resource for your notes, contemplations, or small drawings. At the bottom of the list, add further ones that you know or discover.

Breathe

As a start, take long, slow, deep breaths, inhaling and exhaling evenly. Pay attention to the sensation of your breath moving in and out of your nose. If you are feeling drained and low in energy and need to refresh your system, inhale a bit longer than you exhale. If you are feeling anxious, nervous, or overstimulated and need to settle down, exhale twice as long as you inhale.

_____

_____

Ground

Send your energy all the way down to your feet and connect with the ground below you. Imagine your feet are connecting all the way to the core of the earth. Feel your steadiness and rootedness.

_____

_____

Sway or Rock

Give yourself the soothing rhythm of a gentle holding to support you. Sway or rock, letting your weight shift from side to side. Close your eyes and let yourself be rocked by your own rhythm.

_____

_____

Shake

Move the energy of activation and charge through and out of your body. This can be a small micromovement in your chair or a larger expression of the current moving within you. Consciously unwind.

Make Sound

Take a big, open-mouth sigh. Soften your jaw and let sound move up and out of you. Move the sound as deep from your belly as you can instead of from your throat or head. Move tension, fatigue, density, fear, excitement—whatever is present for you—with this sound. You may not even consciously know what you are releasing here. That's okay too. Use sound to release and create more space.

Contact

Place your hands on your body to feel supported and brought back into your own skin, hands on your belly and breathing underneath them. Or place a hand on your belly and the other on your sacrum. Place your hands on your face and support your head with your hands for a moment. Feel your own self-contact. Use this to bring you home to your body. Soften your head toward your heart and pause. Drop in with what feels true. Receive this moment of pausing and being with yourself.

Meditate

If you already have a meditation practice, use it as one of your steady and deep resources. Sit and feel your breath moving. This can also take the form of prayer. Connect to what you consider Source or the Divine.

Track

Turn toward what is happening inside you right now. Allow your inner world to speak to you through your sensory awareness. Identify and name one of the sensations of aliveness happening within you right now.

Additions

External Resources

External resources are the resources you can turn toward in nature and outside yourself as supports to reorient and land in your body and presence. As with the previous list, there is space to take notes between each resource invitation. Read the list and note which resources you may already be making use of in your life, as well as ones you would most like to try. Again, at the bottom of the list, add further ones that you know or discover.

Nature

Attune to the natural world in all ways. Take a walk and feel the breeze on your skin. Notice the quality of seasonal light. Pay attention to a city skyline. Notice the flowers. Appreciate the snow falling on your nose. Jump in a creek. Walk on the beach. Let nature meet your senses.

Nourishment

Eat a nourishing and satisfying meal. Drink water. Have nourishing conversations with those you trust and love. Laugh with friends. Take a shower or bath and wash off the day. Ask for a hug. Lean on a tree. Rest your head in your friend's or partner's lap.

Beauty

Notice what is beautiful to you: a flower or tree; a painting in a museum; your child's laugh; gorgeous written words. Seek what is beautiful, and spend time attending and attuning to it. Let yourself find beauty in small and big ways. Drink it in.

Pleasure

Seeking pleasure is one of the fastest ways to help you feel more alive and present. Find this in the foods you love, the people you love, the fabrics on your skin that feel lovely to you. Sleep in. Stay up late. Listen to music. Sing. Hang out with your pets. Get dressed up for a day. Stay in your pajamas for a day. Give yourself the gift of pleasure, whatever that is. These are not things you have to "earn."

Creativity

Make a collage. Draw. Paint. Stack rocks by the side of the river. Do a project with your children. Bake. Write. Sew. Sing. Write a song. Dance. Make pottery. Color in a coloring book. Wait for the muse to find you. When the feeling of the muse strikes you, listen and follow the energy. Regardless of whether or not you consider yourself an artist, you have creative capacity.

Play

Dance. Do yoga. Get down on the floor and play with your children. Follow them and do what they do. Ride a bike. Play chase or hide-and-seek. Play is the process of moving and engaging for no other reason than that it's fun.

Real-Life Engagement:
Practice Utilizing Your Resources

Said simply, practice and employ your resources. Build a new habit of caring for yourself by committing to intervening in the moments, waves, and cycles of overwhelm and activation. It is first helpful to know if you are best benefited by internal or external resourcing. We all have our unique wiring, tendencies, and impactful life experiences.

1. This week, pick one internal and one external resource to practice. Pay close attention to how each shifts your breathing, energy, mood, and capacity to engage with your life. Next week, do the same with two others. This little experiment will help give you a sense of what is most helpful to you. Take note of which resources work best for you.

2. Make resourcing a part of how you support yourself. The next time you have a challenging day or feel stressed or even activated, choose a resource and see what happens.

3. If you are a therapist, layer in moments of resourcing with your clients. Pause them or feel for a natural moment to help them resource. If you are a movement educator—a dance teacher or yoga instructor—infuse moments of resources into your sequences, pauses for connection and reorientation. Notice the impact it has on your students.

Reflections

WHEN I AM STRESSED, OVERWHELMED, OR ACTIVATED, I TEND TO ...

THESE RESOURCES WORK THE BEST FOR ME:

USING INTERNAL RESOURCES HELPS ME BY ...

USING EXTERNAL RESOURCES HELPS ME BY ...

MY TOP THREE GO-TO RESOURCES ARE:

THIS IS MY COMMITMENT TO MYSELF THROUGH RESOURCES:

RESOURCING MY CLIENTS/STUDENTS HELPS THEM TO ...

CHAPTER 11

Self-Regulation Practices: Working with Big Energy

Being human means having emotions. These include excitement, fear, wonder, disgust, anger, terror, jealousy, desire for pleasure, grief, joy, compassion, contentment, and so much more. Where you come from, what your family was and is like, how you identify and walk through the world, and how the world sees and acculturates you are all tied into what emotions are more or less appropriate to experience and express. Despite the many ways your emotive capacity may have been culturally and outwardly defined, when it comes to embodiment and being human, encourage as full a capacity as possible to experience your feelings, whatever they may be. The invitation to a full range of emotional capacity is an invitation to experience energy—to feel charge move in your body. Thus, deepening embodiment invites us to expand both our sensory and emotional repertoires as expressions of the energy living within us.

Big Energy

When you begin a process of emotional, psychological, or physical healing and repair, undoubtedly, feelings will arise. Waves of big emotions will surface. Learning to ride the waves of big energy is a two-purpose project. One, it is a necessary part of any healing journey. Two, it is part of the ever-expanding embodiment journey. In regard to the former, healing from all wounds, especially trauma, requires that in some way the pain or activation of that wound or trauma be felt or reexperienced in service of building a new imprint of health. We must feel the impact of the wound in order to heal it.[83] The danger, though, in thawing what has been frozen, in allowing yourself to feel more intensity and even some of the pain of both the original and residual hurt, is in simply recapitulating the wound rather than repairing it. The aim of body-centered healing and all forms of embodied repair is to utilize your felt sense—your actual bodily account and your concurrent feelings and thoughts—as a way to express what has been repressed and create a new pathway.[84] This might look like finally allowing sound to move through your throat and voice that has been previously denied. It might look like realizing certain boundaries must be renegotiated for safety and sanity. It might look like imagining the presence of a helpful supportive other at the time of traumatic impact. It can look like that long-held cry and wail of pent-up grief. In all of these, we stay connected to the felt sense of our body through movement as we merge it with the consciousness of our feeling states. This is the essence of trauma repair, of wound healing, of returning to wholeness, of reweaving the parts of yourself that have been frayed and fragmented.

In relationship to riding waves of big energy as a general life skill—if you are to live a full-spectrum life, with fully embodied emotional experiences in which no part of you is left behind or cut off, then be prepared to feel more. Be prepared for all kinds of energy to move through you. This is a good thing. This is a blessing. Having a strong boat to navigate the sea of life is useful. Skills such as self-regulation, resourcing, and orienting to pleasure support your journey of wholeness, wellness, and embodiment.[85] There is no living without big impact or big energy. Dare to develop the capacity to feel, process, and integrate all of it with greater grace and efficiency.

In the previous chapter, you learned about resources. Building and maintaining an active connection to your resources is critical to being present with big energy, as well as skillfully continuing to regenerate as you move through any large process or transition in your life. Refer to the previous chapter's concepts and prompts for ideas of which resources to choose as a way for you to titrate experience and facilitate greater self-regulation—both of which you will learn and explore here.

Self-Regulation

Self-regulation is your capacity to ride waves of emotion and feeling, to self-soothe in times of discomfort, and to ground yourself during difficulty.[86] It is the ability to discern urgent needs from those that can wait. It is the ability to calm your nervous system and connect to yourself and your world in the face of activation.[87]

Self-regulation is a developmental task. It is learned over time. It is directly linked to the ability to self-soothe your urgency and discomfort. Think of toddlers who all of a sudden throw a tantrum. They are overwhelmed and learning how to express themselves and communicate effectively. They are throwing a tantrum because they do not have other skills yet. They are learning those skills depending on how their caregivers meet them in those moments. You learned them as your caregivers met you in those moments.

Now think of the difference between a toddler and an adult. We expect adults to have the capacity to weather the storm, to identify what is going on for them and how urgent their needs might be. We expect adults to be able to calm themselves and self-soothe when they get frustrated. Yet I'm sure you have plenty of examples in your life of adults who are stunted in this capacity. They can't tolerate discomfort and they explode, or they sneak around to get what they want and need, pretending outwardly that everything is okay. Or they shut down and express very little. Maybe you already have the capacity to self-regulate. Maybe you could use some skill building. Regardless of where you are currently in relation to this capacity or why you need to up your self-regulation game, as an adult you get to cultivate this skill now and always.

Trauma of all kinds makes it very difficult to self-regulate.[88] In fact, that is one of the hallmarks of trauma. It reduces one's capacity to self-soothe and self-regulate. Building self-regulation and self-soothing capacity inherently involves repairing wounds you may have incurred in your earlier development when the skills for healthy and effective self-regulation fell short.[89] If you are going through a particularly challenging time in your life having more recently incurred trauma, such as a traumatic birth of your child, loss of a loved one, assault, a car accident, or discovery of infidelity, you may find that your ability to self-regulate and self-soothe becomes greatly challenged. Perhaps you were able to access supporting yourself much more easily before, but given the current circumstances of your life and process you find such inner tending more difficult. This is normal. It is also an invitation toward greater nourishing resources, deep rest, orientation to pleasure, and asking for help. It is a call to titrate and ride the waves.

Real-Life Engagement:
Practice Self-Regulating Big Energy

These exercises are intended to support you not only through surges of big energy but also when you are going through more prolonged periods of stress. They are also good vitamins for your regular well-being and health.

Yield and ground in nature. Spend some time barefoot on the earth. You can walk on the grass or on the beach. As your feet connect to the earth, feel the textures underneath them and allow the energy of the ground beneath you to charge your battery, so to speak. Feel the earth supporting you and restoring your buoyancy. Lying on the ground is a gorgeous practice. Lie belly down or on your back, depending on what is most comfortable for your body. Allow your body's weight to fully soften, yield, and surrender to the ground. Feel the earth receive you. Give the earth all that you have been processing and feeling. Gather energy and nourishment from the earth's steady strength. Let it renew any places of depletion. If tears come, let the earth have them. If joy arises, let it. Be with it all, the earth as your witness.

Yield into support indoors. Not everyone has access to nature in the same ways. If you live in a place where being safely in nature is not an accessible option, please care for yourself by finding access points for a sense of grounding even when inside. Use this exercise to support your grounding when indoors. Find a comfortable place to lie down. Imagine the soft, grassy earth beneath you, holding you, supporting you. Settle, sink, yield toward the vast and full holding of the earth's embrace. Let your weight drop down, and drop down a bit more. Imagine any places of overwhelm—the parts that feel too much and where it feels too big to hold—all draining like a faucet out of your being and into the earth. Let your emotions move. Imagine the earth soaking up your excess charge and energy like water.

Now imagine the earth rising to meet you and recharging you with buoyancy, support, and aliveness. With your mind's eye, imagine golden sunlight coming up through your toes, into your ankles and legs, then into your hips and pelvis, following up into your belly, and golden light streaming through your whole torso. With each breath, breathe in this golden sunlike quality into your chest and through your arms, up your throat and across your eyes. Let it penetrate behind your eyes and soften the back of your head, finding its way all the way through your crown. Let this imagery and practice be one that sustains your overall process. Return to it again and again.

Postures of Self-Soothing. Come to a child's pose and make a little pillow for your forehead with your hands. Rest your forehead down onto your stacked hands and consciously slow your breath down. Feel your body's weight and allow the full weight of your head to rest. Imagine letting your whole brain rest. Now lift your torso so you are kneeling with your knees wide like with child's pose. Place your left hand and support the back of your head. Place your right hand on your forehead. Use this holding to gently support your head and soften your thinking. Let your hands support the weight of your head as you lean it back into your left hand a little. Use your right hand to gently press down on your forehead skin toward your eyes, further quieting your brain.

Reflections

WRITE DOWN WHAT IT FELT LIKE TO NOURISH YOURSELF IN THIS WAY. NOTE ANY CHANGES IN YOUR FELT SENSE EXPERIENCE, IN THE QUALITY OF YOUR THOUGHTS, IN YOUR PRESENCE.

Titration

In the realms of psychotherapy and trauma healing, we use the term *titration* to describe the process of dipping into a space of activation, followed by a time of integration, in order to support the process of unwinding and repairing trauma.[90] Titration is a chemistry term referring to the mixing of two different substances to make a new, third substance. If the different substances are mixed too quickly, the third substance cannot form. Rather, the two different substances must be added together one drop at a time so they can merge, calibrate, and create the new third substance. Oscillating between activation and integration allows one's system to recalibrate as it experiences healing and finds new homeostasis. Titration is the balance between processing and resourcing, working and resting, experiencing and integrating. This principle helps us navigate big energy. Meeting big emotions head-on without wavering is a nearly impossible task. Titration as a practice invites you into finding your own pacing during intensity and giving yourself room to experience without getting flooded, thereby allowing for real and lasting change.

Imagine you are in a room and suddenly, without warning, the lights go out and you are in the dark. It may take you a few moments to even realize that you are in the dark. Once you do, you fumble to find the light switch, tripping over any items strewn on the floor. Once the light is on, you can resume what you were doing before the lights went out, but you also have to clean up all the things you knocked over on your way to the light switch. This is what it's like to get triggered or activated.

Now imagine that you are in that room and the lights go off and you realize it right away. Imagine that you can sense when the lights are going to go out before they do, and you can say, "Hey, honey, please keep the light on for me, okay?" This is what it is like to work your way backward, tracking the moment you get triggered so that you stay so close to yourself all the time that you know what to ask for.

One of the trickiest yet important keys to capture when you become activated is the moment when it actually occurs. Becoming a witness to the exact moment you go from being engaged to being checked out or freaked out is critical. This is a point at which you can learn to be your best advocate for your own healing journey and expanded self-regulation capacity. Obviously, we won't be perfect at this all the time. But we do get better and more skillful over time.

Real-Life Engagement:
Practice Titration

These exercises and prompts are for you to build your self-regulation bandwidth by helping you identify when you get triggered, supporting you through waves of big energy, and teaching you to advocate for a pacing that allows for sustainable change, growth, and healing in your process.

Track yourself in the moment of activation. What sensations are present when you get triggered? Heat, sweaty palms, mind racing, increased heart rate, confusion, feeling like you might explode or you want to run. Notice if you find yourself saying "Never mind" or "Let's just talk about it later" or "It's fine" or "Forget it." Do you get really tired or spaced out? Do you suddenly realize you must have spaced out or gone somewhere else for a moment? Are all hints you are triggered.

Reflections

WHEN I AM TRIGGERED, I ...

_____

_____

_____

THE MOMENT I GET ACTIVATED FEELS LIKE ...

_____

_____

_____

THIS IS WHAT ACTIVATION FEELS LIKE IN MY BODY:

_____

_____

_____

Work toward sensing when overwhelm is coming. Pay close attention to those moments leading up to realizing the lights went out and you are in the dark. What happens in your body as the sense of overwhelm rises, as the momentum and urgency of activation increase?

_____

_____

_____

I CAN TELL I AM STARTING TO GET OVERWHELMED BECAUSE ...

_____

_____

THESE ARE SOME COMMON TRIGGERS FOR ME:

_____

_____

Take a time-out in difficult conversations. Once you can identify that you are triggered or know when you are getting close to the lights going out, it becomes your responsibility to slow things down. You can ask for time. You can say honestly that you are overwhelmed and need a moment or need help. Make this a practice of noticing your inner state and asking for what you need to regulate.

Reflections

I CAN ASK FOR A TIME-OUT BY SAYING...

ASKING FOR A PAUSE IN A DIFFICULT CONVERSATION HELPS ME TO...

WHEN I AM TRIGGERED AND NEED SOME SPACE TO COME BACK TO MYSELF, MY BODY FEELS...

What to Say to Yourself When You Get Activated

With awareness comes responsibility. If you realize you are triggered or are feeling that tipping point coming on, try the following.

I encourage you to place your hands on your heart or your belly when you say any of these to yourself.

- *This is me being activated.*

- *Wow. Okay. I'm triggered.*

- *This is me in my sadness.*

- *Here is my anger.*

- *This is what terror feels like.*

- *This is a really big emotion/charge.*

- *Whoa, that energy is really big in me.*

What to Say in a Challenging Conversation or Experience with Someone

- *I can tell I'm getting overwhelmed, and I just need a moment to collect myself before we continue.*

- *Wow, I'm feeling so angry hearing/seeing that. I'm going to sit over here for a minute.*

- *This conversation/experience is difficult for me.*

- *I'm overwhelmed. Could you stop talking for a minute and just sit with me?*

- *Can we take a break for twenty minutes?*

What to Do When You Are Activated

- *Name the big energy or feeling.*

- *Connect with a resource that works, whether it is internal or external. Breathe, shake, lie on the floor, take a walk, drink water, make contact with your own body, pay attention to simple details around you, like the color of the wall or the sound of a bird. Give yourself the time to really do this and feel its supportive impact.*

- *Return to the conversation or task when you are ready.*

- *Repeat as a wave arises.*

Reflections

ONCE I KNOW I AM ACTIVATED, THESE ARE MY GO-TO RESOURCES TO SLOW THINGS DOWN AND FIND MY GROUND AGAIN:

_____

_____

_____

ASKING FOR A PAUSE IN A DIFFICULT SITUATION HELPS ME TO ...

_____

_____

_____

THIS IS ME ACKNOWLEDGING MY ACTIVATION:

_____

_____

_____

THIS IS ME ASKING FOR AND SEEKING RESPONSIBLE SUPPORT:

_____

_____

_____

BEING WELL RESOURCED IN THE FACE OF DIFFICULTY FEELS LIKE ...

_____

_____

_____

Orienting to Pleasure and Gratitude

When I was processing the wake of my partner's infidelity, I spent most of my days oscillating between deep grief and consuming rage. It was exhausting. The level of processing and the size of the energy moving in my psyche and in my body were massive. I began with sincerity, for maybe the first time in my life, a practice of pleasure and gratitude. I allowed myself to seek beauty every day: choosing a favorite fabric to wear; looking up at the sky in awe; noticing the very specific gorgeous details of the snow falling; finding the voices of my friends as beautiful as any symphony. I let myself do what I wanted (within healthy reason) for the first time in years, not so much in an adolescent "I can do whatever I want" sort of way, but more in an "I am listening to my instincts, impulses, and desires" kind of way. This was revolutionary. Noting three things I was grateful for each day, despite my despair and heartbreak, kept me sane and oriented to a life whose structures and beliefs were falling apart at the seams.

Pleasure, beauty, and gratitude are part of our birthright and can be found even in small ways during unlikely times. It is part of being embodied. We are designed not just to feel pain and discomfort but also to feel good. Trauma of all kinds, addiction, obsession, disease, and stress all disrupt this innate capacity. Give yourself permission to feel pleasure, no matter how small, to find gratitude, no matter how small. Let this be a part of your embodied healing and evolution, both as a life practice and as a way to ride the waves of any reparative journey. Orienting to pleasure and gratitude is not an invitation to ignore what is difficult. Nor is it permission to excuse yourself from hard work and discomfort. It is, however, a balance maker—a way to keep us whole even when we feel broken, a reminder to find even the smallest glimmers of hope in intense times. Practicing pleasure and gratitude fills our cup even when it is painful to walk to the well and gather the water.

In the previous chapter, we discussed orienting to pleasure and cultivating gratitude even when difficult as invitations of healthy resourcing. Many of us, especially those with trauma, are programmed to withstand and endure more so than listening to instincts and desire. The idea of fun for fun's sake or pleasure because it's simply delicious is foreign, scary, and even dangerous. Challenging this belief safely and unwinding your resistance to pleasure is a worthy process on its own. It is also one way to titrate difficult and painful experiences as they are happening or after they have occurred.

Creative Exercise:
Practice Orienting to Pleasure and Gratitude

Use these two practices below to support you in orienting to pleasure and gratitude as a resource through difficulty.

Keep a gratitude journal. Write down three things you are grateful for every day, no matter how small or silly. Start here and now.

TODAY I AM GRATEFUL FOR ...

_____

_____

_____

Do at least one thing that is pleasurable to you every day. Make this a practice. It might sound counterintuitive, but especially in times of big change or process, stay connected to pleasure.

THIS IS WHAT BROUGHT ME PLEASURE TODAY:

_____

_____

_____

ALLOWING MYSELF TO ORIENT TO BEAUTY AND PLEASURE IS ...

_____

_____

_____

ORIENTING TO PLEASURE IS SCARY OR WEIRD BECAUSE ...

_____

_____

_____

AS I ALLOW MYSELF TO FEEL MORE PLEASURE AND FIND BEAUTY, I AM NOTICING ...

CHAPTER 12

Facing Resistance and Your Inner Critic

In this chapter, we'll explore the concepts of resistance and the inner critic. You'll be guided to explore how they manifest somatically for you. You will also be guided through practices to unstick the power of the inner critic and to find supportive ways to meet and unwind resistance.

The Inner Critic

The *inner critic* is the voice inside you that speaks negatively in harsh judgment. It is the voice that tells you that you are stupid, incapable, falling short, or unlikely to succeed. It is the voice that continually finds fault with the work of others. That says all the ways they should have done things better. The inner critic can show up during deadlines and in social gatherings, in the way we speak to ourselves about our progress and decisions, and in the ways we treat our partners, friends, colleagues, and children. If we were raised by a critical caregiver, we have likely adopted and internalized this criticism through our own self-talk and in how we relate.[91]

This voice often goes hand in hand with perfectionism. A part of us believes that we must find the perfect solution, complete projects perfectly, find the perfect outfit, and make exacting and perfect decisions. The irony of the marriage between criticism and perfectionism is that perfection is an always moving target we often seek in hopes of avoiding disappointment and disapproval—even criticism. As a result, we internalize and take all that critical judgment inward, where it becomes a rather insidious and cruel taskmaster. The more perfection we seek, the more critical we get.[92]

The inner critic has tremendous power and can act in sneaky ways, making you believe things that aren't fully true. It can take over before you even realize this voice is running the show instead of that more integrated, attuned part of yourself.[93] Remember that embodiment means to become that very thing at hand. What if you risked fully embodying the voice of your inner critic? What if you gave that part of yourself permission to speak and run through you? I am not condoning needlessly beating yourself up with negative self-talk. Rather, I suggest that if we are to know ourselves fully—if we are to expand the repertoire of our somatic and emotional capacity—we can make room for this voice to have a seat at our inner dialogue table and recognize it simply as one voice, not the whole truth. We can thereby gain insight into what the inner critic is avoiding, hiding, or fearing. We can also glean insight into the inner critic's roots—where it originated—thereby helping ourselves to hand it back over to where we gathered it.

Creative Exercise:
Practice Embodying Your Inner Critic

In a safe place for you to move, conjure your inner critic's voice. This might look like bringing to mind a common repeated phrase, or it might be a general mood or attitude. As you conjure and connect to your inner critic, begin to walk around your space. This is a simple walk; walk with the attitude of your inner critic. As you walk, notice what it feels like to embody this critical side of yourself. Are you walking fast or slow? With big or small steps? Allow this walking to bring your inner critic to the surface. If you have the impulse to move in any other way, to make any other gestures, or to make sounds, let yourself. Notice what sounds you make, what gestures and other movements or shapes are conjured by embodying this part of yourself.

Reflections

WALKING AS MY INNER CRITIC FEELS ...

_____

_____

_____

THIS IS WHAT MY INNER CRITIC SAYS WHEN I EMBODY HIM/HER/THEM:

_____

_____

_____

WHEN I AM BEING CRITICAL OF MYSELF, MY BODY FEELS ...

_____

_____

_____

WHEN I FIND MYSELF BEING CRITICAL OF SOMEONE AROUND ME, MY BODY FEELS ...

_____

_____

_____

MY INNER CRITIC FEELS LIKE _____ IN MY BODY. IT SOUNDS LIKE _____. IT MAKES ME FEEL _____.

_____

_____

_____

Journal Inquiry:
Practice Befriending Your Inner Critic

Once you have a clear grasp of the way your inner critic feels and sounds like, you can begin to confront it with patient ferocity. I say *patient ferocity* because the inner critic often guards something sensitive to us—a vulnerability or fear, a sadness, an unmet need. This requires patience and compassion to work with. The inner critic is a coping mechanism for the vulnerability that lives beneath perfectionism. So, confronting the inner critic also means meeting what it guards. It requires ferocity because the inner critic is often seductive. Your boundaries need to be clear that this critic can be included but is not in charge.

After you have evoked and embodied your inner critic by walking the walk of its attitude, ask it these questions directly. Let your inner critic answer.

WHAT IS IT THAT YOU ARE FEELING CRITICAL ABOUT?

WHAT IS IT THAT YOU SEE HAPPENING AROUND YOU?

WHAT IS IT THAT YOU ARE MOST NEEDING?

WHAT GUIDANCE DO YOU HAVE FOR ME?

Take a moment of reflection, integration, and movement to incorporate the answers into your soma. Perhaps you realized that your inner critic truly needs permission to be messy. Perhaps your inner critic is showing you where you need understanding. Perhaps it's pointing you toward seeing an injustice. Options for incorporation of these truths include making a shape with your body to receive its impact; rocking or swaying to bring the truth into your being; shaking your body to make room for these insights; doing a yoga posture that helps you imbibe the impact of the truthful answer.

Resistance

Simply put, *resistance* is that which is not yet ready to change. Often resistance means that something—be it an emotion, an expression, a movement, or a relationship dynamic—is stuck and needs support if it is to move.[94] It is the wall that keeps us outside of deepening and expanding into the next possible iteration. It hangs out on the precipice of vulnerability, keeping us closer to what we think is more comfortable, even if it is less than optimal. Resistance is a phenomenal teacher of boundaries and safety. It may serve to remind us of a boundary, denoting a need that must be addressed before we can proceed. It can signal the need for a recommitment to and reassurance of safety before we deepen into the next phase of a relationship or emotional exploration. Resistance also shows us where our willpower has become rigid—where we are powering through and attempting stoicism—when what we truly need is empowerment and support to be fully who and where we are.

For me personally, though working with resistance both inside myself and with others is challenging, it is always rewarding and beckons me toward deeper intimacy. I have learned to never force the door of resistance open. *Pushing past resistance* is an unhelpful ubiquitous phrase linked to the perfectionist agenda, which can turn us back toward our inner critic instead of toward patient, generative empowerment. I prefer to pay my respects to resistance by honoring its presence and staying close to its needs. Often, when I welcome it, I find resistance is less of a threat to progress and change and more of a guardian at the gate of possibility. It shows me what needs to happen, what needs to soften, what needs reassurance and patience before more vulnerability can be had.

In our bodies, we might feel resistance to movement or rest. We may experience literal resistance in our bodies to specific movements, a range of motion, or a stretch. Resistance can show up emotionally, subverting one's ability to be present with a difficult emotion. It can show up as a protective mechanism to counter vulnerability in relationships. Suffice to say, resistance deserves our respect more than our force. It deserves deep listening rather than judgment, curious inquiry rather than conflictual engagement.

Real-Life Engagement:
Practice Meeting Resistance

Below you will practice and explore meeting your resistance through movement and in relationships. The aim here is for you to get well-acquainted with how your resistance shows up in you so that it is more conscious and, thereby, possible for you to make shifts.

In movement. Meet the ways resistance shows up in your body during any movement practice. Pay attention to what is happening internally. Is there tension as you move? If so, where? Does your body feel limited? When, how, where? Describe what physical resistance in your body feels like. How do you react to the feeling of resistance in your physicality? Do you push through? Do you give up? Can you come up next to the sense of resistance, let it be okay, and move in conjunction with it rather than against it?

Reflections

RESISTANCE IN MY BODY OFTEN FEELS LIKE ...

MY NORMAL RESPONSE TO MY PHYSICAL RESISTANCE IS ...

THIS IS HOW I CAN SOFTEN MY PHYSICAL RESISTANCE:

In relationships. Meet your resistance by paying attention to how and when it shows up in your relationships. Where in your life do you feel resistance? When this arises in your daily life, what happens in your body? What posture do you take? Do you become sharp and frustrated? Do you shrink back? What does relational resistance look and feel like in your body?

Reflections

WHEN I HAVE RESISTANCE TO A PERSON, CONVERSATION, OR PLACE, MY BODY ...

_____

_____

_____

THIS IS WHERE I FEEL RESISTANCE IN MY LIFE RIGHT NOW:

_____

_____

_____

Creative Exercise:
Practice Befriending Your Resistance

1) To befriend the resistance you feel, use this self-talk to name, honor, and accept it. Say these statements to yourself. Notice how they impact you. Which ones feel the most powerful and true to you? Why?

- I can feel how strong this resistance is.

- I am not ignoring this resistance. I am right here with it.

- I am not going to push this resistance away or make it bad.

- I honor my resistance, and it is okay.

Reflections

2) Now ask your resistance what it needs, what it is guarding, and what might assuage it. This is quite similar to the work you did with your inner critic.

WHAT IS IT THAT YOU ARE GUARDING?

_____

_____

WHERE IS IT THAT YOU NEED TO FIND SOME FLOW?

_____

_____

WHAT WOULD BE SUPPORTIVE RIGHT NOW?

_____

_____

_____

3) Support your resistance in unwinding with this movement practice.

Take a very wide stance, turn your feet out, and bend your knees. Place your hands somewhere on your thighs. Some of you will recognize this as goddess pose. Essentially you are in a wide squat with your toes and knees turned out. Feel the strength in your legs as you use your arms and hands to push down on your thighs and stretch your spine up and away from your hips. On the rhythm of your breath, exhale, taking your left shoulder toward your right knee. Inhale to come back to the center. Exhale your right shoulder toward your left knee. Inhale back to the center. Repeat this for a few rounds. Feel the strength in your legs and the turning in your belly, spine, and insides. If you feel like exhaling with an open-mouth sigh, go for it.

Come back to the center, release your arms down in front of you, and let them swing and dangle naturally as you hold the wide squat position. Use your breath to release resistant energy. Inhale as fully as you can. On your exhale, shake, release, and dangle your arms toward the floor in front of you. Let yourself sigh and make sounds on the exhale as you release your arms. Do this a few times, letting yourself release the resistance in your heart or your mind.

Bring your feet back together and stand tall but soft. See if any energy is freed up. Practice a bit of rocking and swaying rhythm to ground and nourish yourself. Let the places of resistance residue untangle and smooth as you invite a flowing quality. Move as an unimpeded river would. If it feels like there is more stagnant or resistant energy remaining, feel free to repeat the previous exercise. Then come back to a bit of flow once more.

Lying down comfortably, place your hands on the part of your body that feels resistant or stuck. If it is emotional, place your hands on your heart or belly or on a place that helps you contact the emotion. With a very gentle and loving quality of touch, simply keep your hand on the part of your body that needs attention in its resistance. Allow it to receive this attention. Let the resistance here be known and acknowledged.

Reflections

CONTACTING RESISTANCE FEELS ...

WHEN I MOVE RESISTANCE OUT OF MY BODY, I FEEL ...

_____

_____

_____

_____

WHEN I TURN TOWARD MY RESISTANCE INSTEAD OF AWAY FROM IT, THIS HAPPENS:

_____

_____

_____

_____

CHAPTER 13

Including Your Body in Ritual

Rituals, by nature, create sacred space and time.[95] They delineate a container for the numinous to enter, for spirit to enliven the space and thereby us, to bring toward us prayers and messages, to help conjure spirit from within. Rituals name time and space as specific, making it distinct from the rest of the day, week, or year. Rituals can occur directly to and through one's body, such as that in Judaism of the bris, or circumcision for male newborns, and going to the mikvah for females at specific times in their lives. Communion in the Christian faith is the somatic remembrance and embodied practice of honoring the body of Christ. Whether or not you agree with or abide by these religious rites, they are examples of direct somatic rituals that sanctify and distinguish the individual's soma as in the presence of the holy and the Divine. We can take from this the notion that what is sacred and holy is not separate from the body. Naming and bringing forward the holy may happen directly through our own lived experience, reminding us that it is possible not only to include one's body in a ritual but also to create an entire ritual center within the fabric of one's soma.

Although ritual behavior is present in religions and faiths, by no means are these the only places where it can be transmitted, taught, and cultivated. It is powerful to create your own rituals that name sacred time and space. We need not lean only upon the rituals of organized faith. We can use our own somatic intelligence to create meaningful rituals of and for the body. Furthermore, reincorporating your body into any ritual, whether it be from a place of organized faith or your own connection to spirit, can help to enliven and deepen your somatic connection to and experience of the divine. Especially if you have places of pain, persecution, or trauma from religious faith and practice, bringing your body back into it on your own terms can be incredibly empowering and healing. There are a few key components to any body-based ritual: gesture, movement, and somatic receiving of impact. As you find ways to both incorporate your body into rituals and create body-based rituals, consider these components as guides.

Gesture

Making symbolic and representational gestures with your hands can be a beautiful and meaningful way to externalize what is in your heart. It can help you in your ritualized space in a few ways: setting and symbolizing intention, externalizing what you are putting into or taking from the ritual, marking points throughout the ritual, and showing impact of the ritual. In the yogic traditions, the practice of gesture is called *mudra*. Mudra is a way that materializes and expresses what is internal.[96] In the yogic tradition I have personally studied, mudras serve as a way to embody teachings, states of mind, qualities of the divine, or even the essence of a prayer. They reveal and tell a story, encapsulating rich meanings with just a few finger movements. They are contained little worlds held within one's hands that link an idea, quality, or prayer with one's hands, heart, and brain. They represent in small, tangible ways what is ineffable. Mudra is a method of imprinting consciousness.

The practice of mudra is specific and intricate. It takes quite a bit of time to master. Even if you have not studied this very specific practice, you can use the notion of mudra as inspiration to create your own intuitive gestures to express the intentions, experience, and reverence of your ritual. The shapes made with and through your hands are microcosms of the wider scope, small embodiments of large ideas, like a seed that holds the encoded possibility of the flower to bloom. They invoke the intention of the practice or ritual. The invitation here is to follow your instinct and impulse to make shapes and gestures with your hands that speak to and from you into the ritualized space. Let your hands be truly inspired, taking what is in your heart and expressing it outwardly. Make symbols. Let your consciousness unfold itself through your hands. Let your hands be the doorway from the ritual back into your body, heart, and mind. Feel free to practice just this right now.

Close your eyes and take a few breaths. Let the words about gesture and ritual sink into your system. Now, without overthinking, make a gesture with your hands that represents your experience right now. Hold that gesture for a few breaths, allowing your whole body to receive its imprint. Pay attention to what gesture you made.

Movement

I remember being a child in synagogue, a bit bored and disconnected and trying to look as if I were paying attention. I found watching people pray to be a fascinating experience, honestly more engaging than the actual praying itself. I watched the way people swayed, rocked, clapped, leaned, closed their eyes, lifted or bowed their heads as they prayed. I paid particular attention to the embodied gestures of the service components, such as the way we faced, when we stood or sat, even particular steps and gestures we took with certain prayers. Movement, ritual, and prayer seem, to me, inextricably linked. Have you ever found that you may not remember a prayer's exact words, but the simple gesture that coincides with its recitation somehow jogs your memory and body into knowing? Have you ever found yourself swaying or rocking when singing or praying? Have you found yourself moved by the melody and the recitation?

I'll admit I am not an avid synagogue goer. That said, I pray a lot. I pray with my body, mostly. Often when I need to create a space to commune with spirit it is directly through moving my body. I do this primarily through yoga and free-form dance. As you go about generating creative and meaningful embodied rituals for yourself in your life, consider how your body moves and is moved with your prayers, intentions, and offerings. Whether you are connected to any kind of religious background or not, your body and your embodied expression are a direct line to spirit. They are a direct pathway for the movement of any ritual. Your ritual can happen completely and entirely through your body, or moving your body can be a component of a larger ritual. Discover ways to bring your moving body into the ritual space. Move as you recite a prayer. Attune to the embodied experience of the ritual rites.

Receiving Impact

As you already know, moving your body opens up a pathway to hear your innermost self. It uncovers what needs to be seen, felt, received, listened to, and honored. As you hear these messages bubble up or stream in, let your body move in response. You might find you come to bow on your knees or lie down on the floor. You may find you shake your body or stomp your feet. You may find you pulse or rock or sway. Let your body receive the full impact here.

Practice Tuning into the Somatic Experience of Ritual

This is really just an invitation to bring your whole self to the table when experiencing a ritual. Let your body be moved throughout the ritual. Let yourself sway or rock. Let yourself move to song. There is no need to hold yourself in any rigid position for the sake of honoring spirit. Let yourself be moved, inspired, and impacted as you go through the ritual steps. Stay open and curious to what can move through you when you soften to the idea that your body is allowed to move as prayers are said, songs are sung, gestures are made, and rituals are conducted.

Movement Exercises:
Practice Infusing Movement into the Ritual

After you open a ritual space and set the intention for the ritual, spend three to five minutes moving your body. This can be to a song you choose. It can be quietly stretching and breathing. It can be a few sun salutations or yoga postures. Bring yourself into your body as fully as possible. You can place movement into any portion of a ritual you see fit.

Practice Gesture and Shape

Close your ritual by making three shapes with your body. Think of this as a whole-body gesture. The first shape is a gesture to embody what you are receiving from this ritual. The second shape is a whole-body gesture of what you are offering to the world as a result of this ritual, how you are paying the ritual forward. The third shape is to close and seal the ritual, to say thank you with your whole body, to find meaningful closure with your whole body.

How to Create a Movement Ritual

The following is simply a template—a scaffolding of suggestions for you to embellish as you create a movement-based ritual. Use what is useful to you. You may choose to include movement practices in which you are already well versed. Bring in prayers from your own lineage. Whether the ritual is seasonal or cyclical, denotes a life transition, or is a daily reverent practice, let yourself be inspired.

Create the space. Ritual space is a space that denotes a particular place and time. Ritual space invites liminal space and time where communion with spirit—be it internal, external, or both—can occur. It says that spirit is invited. Prayers will unfold. Make your space special. But no elaborate tools are necessary here. One candle will do, or a stick of incense, a picture of one of your ancestors, a few flowers. If you have none of these things, you can simply tidy up your space and write Ritual Happens Here on a piece of paper. Keep this at the "top" of your space while you move.

Set the intention. Name to yourself (and to others if they are present) the intention of the ritual. What is its purpose? What is the intention? What are you hoping for here? Denote that the ritual is beginning with a gesture of your hands.

Invoke embodiment and spirit. Read a poem or verse. Say a prayer. Let your body move as you do this, should you be inspired.

Move. Begin with a few moments of a grounding practice, and then express the prayer through your body. If you want to move freely, great. If you want to say prayers you already know and let your body move a little bit while you do, great. If you have a yoga practice you would like to do, great. You could also pick one or more of the movement and embodiment practices from this book. If there is an emotion you are trying to move through your body, that is fair game too. This is the time and space to connect with your intention in movement, to move what needs to be offered up, to clear space in your body to receive.

Receive and gather. Once you sense that the movement portion of your ritual is complete, rest as a means to integrate and receive any insight. Write down what emerges from within you. It might be a few words or a phrase. It might be a little drawing. Place your hands on your body and thread any insights back into your being.

Offer thanks. Do this literally. You can say thank you. Place your hands on your heart. Soften your gaze down toward your heart. Offer thanks. Stretch your arms up open and wide, gaze up, and offer thanks. Make a whole-body gesture of gratitude.

Release the ritual. Make a full-body gesture that closes the space. Make a small gesture with your hands that seals the space.

Reflections

BRINGING MY BODY INTO RITUAL FEELS ...

USING MY BODY TO EXPRESS MY PRAYERS IS ...

SINCE BRINGING MY BODY INTO RITUAL SPACE MORE, I HAVE NOTICED ...

KEY INSIGHTS FROM MY BODY RITUALS ARE ...

Closing

My hope is that the information and exercises in this book will continue to enliven you over time. Use these prompts to help inspire your somatic intelligence anytime you may have forgotten. Expand upon the exercises and prompts. Use them as springboards for your teaching and service. If this work has inspired you toward deeper study, follow your curiosity. The field of somatics is vast and includes many entry points. Choose a topic and dive in. A list of further readings is provided in the bibliography.

Remember that embodiment is a birthright. One of the greatest gifts we can give the world is honoring the gift of that birthright by inhabiting our bodies with presence, grace, and dignity. Trauma, addiction, unhealthy behavioral patterns, stress, depression, and dis-ease all take us out of our bodies. To be embodied is to be a feeling being in all ways. This is hard work. No one vacates their body because they want to. They vacate their embodied experience because they learned they could in order to survive. But to thrive, well-being and embodiment are inextricably linked. The wider and fuller our repertoires of emotion, sensing, and moving become, the more *well* we actually are. May these practices move you toward your wellness and wholeness, inspiring others around you to do the same. A friend once said that I help those around me be more of themselves—their whole selves—simply by being myself. I wish this for you. May the gift of your presence innately invite others into safe understanding that they too can come home.

From my body to yours,

Livia

Notes

1   Susan M. Aposhyan, *Natural Intelligence: Body-Mind Integration and Human Development* (Boulder, CO: Now Press, 2007).

2   Bessel Van der Kolk, *The Body Keeps the Score: Brain, Mind, and Body in the Healing of Trauma* (New York: Penguin Books, 2015).

3   Pat Ogden, Kekuni Minton, and Clare Pain, *Trauma and the Body: A Sensorimotor Approach to Psychotherapy* (New York: W. W. Norton, 2006).

4   Peter A. Levine, *Waking the Tiger—Healing Trauma: The Innate Capacity to Transform Overwhelming Experiences* (Berkeley, CA: North Atlantic Books, 1997).

5   Aposhyan, *Natural Intelligence*.

6   Van der Kolk, *Body Keeps the Score*.

7   Aposhyan, *Natural Intelligence*.

8   Merriam-Webster.com Dictionary, s.v. "soma," accessed July 8, 2020, https://www.merriam-webster.com/dictionary/soma.

9   John A. Grimes, *A Concise Dictionary of Indian Philosophy: Sanskrit-English* (Albany: State University of New York Press, 1996).

10   Thomas Hanna, *Somatics: Reawakening the Mind's Control of Movement, Flexibility, and Health* (Cambridge, MA: Da Capo Press, 2004).

11   Bonnie Bainbridge Cohen, Lisa Nelson, and Nancy Stark Smith, *Sensing, Feeling, and Action: The Experiential Anatomy of Body-Mind Centering* (Northampton, MA: Contact Editions, 2003).

12   Christine Caldwell, *Getting Our Bodies Back: Recovery, Healing, and Transformation through Body-Centered Psychotherapy* (Boulder, CO: Shambhala, 1996), 13.

13   Aposhyan, *Natural Intelligence*.

14   Christine Caldwell and Kern Foundation, *Getting in Touch: The Guide to New Body-Centered Therapies* (Wheaton, IL: Quest Books, 1997).

15   Susan M. Aposhyan, *Body-Mind Psychotherapy: Principles, Techniques, and Practical Applications* (New York: W. W. Norton, 2004).

16   Pat Ogden and Janina Fisher, *Sensorimotor Psychotherapy: Interventions for Trauma and Attachment* (New York: W. W. Norton, 2015).

17   Levine, *Waking the Tiger*.

18   Ogden, Minton, and Pain, *Trauma and the Body*.

19   Levine, *Waking the Tiger*.

20   Ann Weiser Cornell, *The Power of Focusing: A Practical Guide to Emotional Self-Healing* (New York: New Harbinger, 1998).

21   Aposhyan, *Body-Mind Psychotherapy*.

22   Caldwell and Kern Foundation, *Getting in Touch*.

23   Martha Hart Eddy, *Mindful Movement: The Evolution of the Somatic Arts and Conscious Action* (Bristol, UK: Intellect, 2017).

24   John O'Donohue, *Anam Ċara: A Book of Celtic Wisdom* (New York: Harper Perennial, 2004).

25   Levine, *Waking the Tiger*, 87.

26   Levine, *Waking the Tiger*.

27   Cohen, Nelson, and Smith, *Sensing, Feeling, and Action*.

28   Levine, *Waking the Tiger*.

29   Carol-Lynne Moore and Kaoru Yamamoto, *Beyond Words: Movement Observation and Analysis* (London: Routledge, 2012).

30   Moore and Yamamoto, *Beyond Words*.

31   Moore and Yamamoto, *Beyond Words*.

32   Aposhyan, *Body-Mind Psychotherapy*.

33   Aposhyan, *Natural Intelligence*.

34   Cohen, Nelson, and Smith, *Sensing, Feeling, and Action*.

35   Janet Kestenberg Amighi, Susan Loman, Penny Lewis, and K. Mark Sossin, *The Meaning of Movement: Embodied Developmental, Clinical, and Cultural Perspectives of the Kestenberg Movement Profile* (London: Routledge, 1999).

36   Cecily Dell, *Space Harmony: Basic Terms* (New York: Dance Notation Bureau Press, 1984).

37   Aposhyan, *Natural Intelligence*.

38   Dell, *Space Harmony*.

39   Aposhyan, *Natural Intelligence*.

40   David J. Wallin, *Attachment in Psychotherapy* (New York: Guilford Press, 2007).

41   Arielle Schwartz, *A Practical Guide to Complex PTSD: Compassionate Strategies to Begin Healing from Childhood Trauma* (Emeryville, CA: Rockridge Press, 2020).

42   Moore and Yamamoto, *Beyond Words*.

43   Aposhyan, *Natural Intelligence*.

44   Helen Payne et al., eds., *The Routledge International Handbook of Embodied Perspectives in Psychotherapy: Approaches from Dance Movement and Body Psychotherapies* (London: Routledge, 2019).

45   Aposhyan, *Natural Intelligence*.

46   Moore and Yamamoto, *Beyond Words*.

47   Payne et al., *Embodied Perspectives in Psychotherapy*.

48   Aposhyan, *Body-Mind Psychotherapy*.

49   Wallin, *Attachment in Psychotherapy*.

50   Amighi et al., *Meaning of Movement*.

51   Aposhyan, *Body-Mind Psychotherapy*.

52   Amighi et al., *Meaning of Movement*.

53   Aposhyan, *Natural Intelligence*.

54   Aposhyan, *Body-Mind Psychotherapy*.

55   Cohen, Nelson, and Smith, *Sensing, Feeling, and Action*.

56   Patrizia Pallaro, ed., *Authentic Movement: A Collection of Essays by Mary Starks Whitehouse, Janet Adler, and Joan Chodorow* (London: Jessica Kingsley, 1999).

57   Van der Kolk, *Body Keeps the Score*.

58   Cohen, Nelson, and Smith, *Sensing, Feeling, and Action*.

59   Ogden and Fisher, *Sensorimotor Psychotherapy*.

60   Levine, *Waking the Tiger*.

61   Caldwell and Kern Foundation, *Getting in Touch*.

62   Aposhyan, *Natural Intelligence*.

63   Edward M. Podvoll, *Recovering Sanity: A Compassionate Approach to Understanding and Treating Psychosis* (Boston: Shambhala, 2003).

64   Gabrielle Roth and John Loudon, *Maps to Ecstasy: The Healing Power of Movement* (Novato, CA: New World Library, 1998).

65   Ida Pauline Rolf and Rosemary Feitis, *Rolfing and Physical Reality* (Rochester, VT: Healing Arts Press, 1990).

66   Ruthie Fraser and Cyndi Lee, *Stack Your Bones: 100 Simple Lessons for Realigning Your Body and Moving with Ease* (New York: The Experiment, 2017).

67   Rolf and Feitis, *Rolfing and Physical Reality*.

68   Caldwell and Kern Foundation, *Getting in Touch*.

69   Amighi et al., *Meaning of Movement*.

70   Cohen, Nelson, and Smith, *Sensing, Feeling, and Action*.

71   Cohen, Nelson, and Smith, *Sensing, Feeling, and Action*.

72   Pallaro, *Authentic Movement*.

73   Levine, *Waking the Tiger*.

74   Ogden and Fisher, *Sensorimotor Psychotherapy*.

75   Pallaro, *Authentic Movement*.

76   Alexander Lowen, *Bioenergetics: The Revolution Therapy That Uses the Language of the Body to Heal the Problems of the Mind* (New York: Arkana, 1994).

77   Cohen, Nelson, and Smith, *Sensing, Feeling, and Action*.

78   Aposhyan, *Natural Intelligence*.

79   Gabrielle Roth, *Sweat Your Prayers: Movement as Spiritual Practice* (Dublin: Newleaf, 1999).

80   Pallaro, *Authentic Movement*.

81   Roth and Loudon, *Maps to Ecstasy*.

82   Levine, *Waking the Tiger*.

83   Van der Kolk, *Body Keeps the Score*.

84   Levine, *Waking the Tiger*.

85   Arielle Schwartz, *The Post-Traumatic Growth Guidebook: Practical Mind-Body Tools to Heal Trauma, Foster Resilience, and Awaken Your Potential* (Eau Claire, WI: PESI, 2020).

86   Allan N. Schore and James S. Grotstein, *Affect Regulation and the Origin of the Self: The Neurobiology of Emotional Development* (London: Routledge, 2016).

87   Louis J. Cozolino, *The Neuroscience of Human Relationships: Attachment and the Developing Social Brain* (New York: W. W. Norton, 2014).

88   Levine, *Waking the Tiger.*

89   Schwartz, *Post-Traumatic Growth Guidebook.*

90   Levine, *Waking the Tiger.*

91   Toko-pa Turner, *Belonging: Remembering Ourselves Home* (Salt Spring Island, British Columbia: Her Own Room Press, 2017).

92   Marion Woodman, *Addiction to Perfection: The Still Unravished Bride* (Toronto: Inner City Books, 1982).

93   Roth and Loudon, *Maps to Ecstasy.*

94   Theresa B. Moyers and Stephen Rollnick, "A Motivational Interviewing Perspective on Resistance in Psychotherapy," *Journal of Clinical Psychology* 58, no. 2 (2002): 185–93, https://doi.org/10.1002/jclp.1142.

95   Mircea Eliade, *The Sacred and the Profane: The Nature of Religion* (New York: Harper & Row, 1961).

96   Cain Carroll, Revital Carroll, and David Frawley, *Mudras of India: A Comprehensive Guide to the Hand Gestures of Yoga and Indian Dance* (Philadelphia: Singing Dragon, 2013).

Bibliography

Amighi, Janet Kestenberg, Susan Loman, and K. Mark Sossin. *The Meaning of Movement: Developmental and Clinical Perspectives of the Kestenberg Movement Profile.* London: Routledge, 1999.

Aposhyan, Susan M. *Body-Mind Psychotherapy: Principles, Techniques, and Practical Applications.* New York: W. W. Norton, 2004.

Aposhyan, Susan M. *Natural Intelligence: Body-Mind Integration and Human Development.* Boulder, CO: Now Press, 2007.

Brook, Annie. *From Conception to Crawling: Foundations for Developmental Movement.* Body-Mind.Net, 2001.

Caldwell, Christine. *Getting Our Bodies Back: Recovery, Healing, and Transformation through Body-Centered Psychotherapy.* Boston: Shambhala, 1996.

Caldwell, Christine, and Kern Foundation. *Getting in Touch: The Guide to New Body-Centered Therapies.* Wheaton, IL: Quest Books, 1997.

Carroll, Cain, Revital Carroll, and David Frawley. *Mudras of India: A Comprehensive Guide to the Hand Gestures of Yoga and Indian Dance.* Philadelphia: Singing Dragon, 2013.

Chevalier, Gaétan. "The Effect of Grounding the Human Body on Mood." *Psychological Reports* 116, no. 2 (2015): 534–42. https://doi.org/10.2466/06.pr0.116k21w5.

Cohen, Bonnie Bainbridge, Lisa Nelson, and Nancy Stark Smith. *Sensing, Feeling, and Action: The Experiential Anatomy of Body-Mind Centering.* Northampton, MA: Contact Editions, 2003.

Cornell, Ann Weiser. *The Power of Focusing: A Practical Guide to Emotional Self-Healing.* New York: New Harbinger, 1998.

Cozolino, Louis J. *The Neuroscience of Human Relationships: Attachment and the Developing Social Brain.* New York: W. W. Norton, 2014.

Cozolino, Louis J. *The Neuroscience of Psychotherapy: Building and Rebuilding the Human Brain.* New York: W. W. Norton, 2002.

Dell, Cecily, Aileen Crow, Irmgard Bartenieff, and Dance Notation Bureau. *Space Harmony: Basic Terms.* New York: Dance Notation Bureau Press, 1984.

Eddy, Martha Hart. *Mindful Movement: The Evolution of the Somatic Arts and Conscious Action.* Bristol, UK: Intellect, 2017.

Eliade, Mircea. *The Sacred and the Profane: The Nature of Religion*. New York: Harper & Row, 1961.

Fraser, Ruthie, and Cyndi Lee. *Stack Your Bones: 100 Simple Lessons for Realigning Your Body and Moving with Ease*. New York: The Experiment, 2017.

Grimes, John A. *A Concise Dictionary of Indian Philosophy: Sanskrit-English*. Albany: State University of New York Press, 1996.

Hanna, Thomas. *Somatics: Reawakening the Mind's Control of Movement, Flexibility, and Health*. Cambridge, MA: Da Capo Press, 2004.

Levine, Peter A. *Waking the Tiger—Healing Trauma: The Innate Capacity to Transform Overwhelming Experiences*. Berkeley, CA: North Atlantic Books, 1997.

Lowen, Alexander. *Bioenergetics: The Revolutionary Therapy That Uses the Language of the Body to Heal the Problems of the Mind*. New York: Arkana, 1994.

Michaels, Melissa. *Youth on Fire: Birthing a Generation of Embodied Global Leaders*. Boulder, CO: Golden Bridge, 2017.

Moore, Carol-Lynne, and Kaoru Yamamoto. *Beyond Words: Movement Observation and Analysis*. London: Routledge, 2012.

Moyers, Theresa B., and Stephen Rollnick. "A Motivational Interviewing Perspective on Resistance in Psychotherapy." *Journal of Clinical Psychology* 58, no. 2 (2002): 185–93. https://doi.org/10.1002/jclp.1142.

O'Donohue, John. *Anam Ċara: A Book of Celtic Wisdom*. New York: Harper Perennial, 2004.

Ogden, Pat, and Janina Fisher. *Sensorimotor Psychotherapy: Interventions for Trauma and Attachment*. New York: W. W. Norton, 2015.

Ogden, Pat, Kekuni Minton, and Clare Pain. *Trauma and the Body: A Sensorimotor Approach to Psychotherapy*. New York: W. W. Norton, 2006.

Pallaro, Patrizia, ed. *Authentic Movement: A Collection of Essays by Mary Starks Whitehouse, Janet Adler, and Joan Chodorow*. London: Jessica Kingsley, 1999.

Payne, Helen, Sabine Koch, Jennifer Tantia, and Thomas Fuchs, eds. *The Routledge International Handbook of Embodied Perspectives in Psychotherapy: Approaches from Dance Movement and Body Psychotherapies*. London: Routledge, 2019.

Podvoll, Edward M. *Recovering Sanity: A Compassionate Approach to Understanding and Treating Psychosis*. Boston: Shambhala, 2003.

Rolf, Ida Pauline, and Rosemary Feitis. *Rolfing and Physical Reality*. Rochester, VT: Healing Arts Press, 1990.

Roth, Gabrielle. *Sweat Your Prayers: Movement as Spiritual Practice*. Dublin: Newleaf, 1999.

Roth, Gabrielle, and John Loudon. *Maps to Ecstasy: The Healing Power of Movement*. Novato, CA: New World Library, 1998.

Schore, Allan N., and James S. Grotstein. *Affect Regulation and the Origin of the Self: The Neurobiology of Emotional Development*. London: Routledge, 2016.

Schwartz, Arielle. *The Post-Traumatic Growth Guidebook: Practical Mind-Body Tools to Heal Trauma, Foster Resilience, and Awaken Your Potential*. Eau Claire, WI: PESI, 2020.

Schwartz, Arielle. *A Practical Guide to Complex PTSD: Compassionate Strategies to Begin Healing from Childhood Trauma*. Emeryville, CA: Rockridge Press, 2020.

Turner, Toko-pa. *Belonging: Remembering Ourselves Home*. Salt Spring Island, British Columbia: Her Own Room Press, 2017.

Van der Kolk, Bessel. *The Body Keeps the Score: Brain, Mind, and Body in the Healing of Trauma*. New York: Penguin Books, 2015.

Wallin, David J. *Attachment in Psychotherapy*. New York: Guilford Press, 2007.

Woodman, Marion. *Addiction to Perfection: The Still Unravished Bride*. Toronto: Inner City Books, 1982.

Acknowledgments

Let us pay deep respect and offer thanks. Many people supported the writing of this workbook. From knowledge gathering, creative inspiration, technical advisement, and unseen love and devotion, it is a pleasure to write these words of gratitude to each of you.

Let me first acknowledge and pay homage to the leaders in the fields of somatic psychology, dance movement therapy, trauma healing, and neuroscience, whose shoulders and work I stand directly on. Their seeing eyes and bodies are the very hands that built the work of this field—the foundation upon which this workbook rests. Christine Caldwell, Susan Aposhyan, Bonnie Bainbridge Cohen, Martha Eddy, Mary Starks Whitehouse, Janet Adler, Zoe Avstrei, Irmgard Bartenieff, Rudolph Laban, Janet Kestenberg, Ryan Kennedy, Pat Ogden, Thomas Hanna, Peter Levine, Bessel Van der Kolk, Daniel Siegel, Lois Cozolino, and Arielle Schwartz, thank you for your bushwhacking, creations, and insights.

In addition to these foundations, to my teachers at Naropa University, whose skill sets are directly present in this book, Ryan Kennedy, Christine Caldwell, Leah D'Abate, Wendy Allen, Zoe Avstrei, and Julie Dolan, and my exceptional first teachers who taught me how to write, Rebecca Hanson and Leslie Rosen, thank you for the container for this book.

My foundational understanding of somatics and the very roots of my embodied practice come from the yoga lineage. Great thanks to my brilliant teachers along the way: Robyn Katz, Piper Petrie, John Friend, Mitchel and Tracy Bleier, Donna Jackson, Christina Sell, Jeanie Manchester, Cindy Lusk, Douglas Brooks, and Paul Muller-Ortega. Your lifelong dedications to the teaching and practices of yoga have gifted me an abundance of lived and learned experiences I cherish.

To my esteemed yoga colleagues, who began a tiny experiment with me years ago, learning to infuse the teaching of yoga with the principles and teachings of somatic psychology, thank you for your inspiration, colleagueship, and studentship. Your direct participation changed my life.

Melissa Michaels, Hannah Loewenthal, and Gabrielle Roth, thank you always and forever for the Dance. For the practice of wild sanity and deep curiosity. May the beat of your teachings pulse outward from this book.

Taryn Toomey and the teachers of The Class, thank you for the method of your embodied practices, for the container for self-study and deep processing you provided me in my tiny corner of the world during the quarantine that was writing this book. You have my sincere and deep respect for what you have created. Please keep going.

Deep gratitude to Ashten Evans of Ulysses Press, who found me by chance and took a leap on a first-time author for this workbook and for helping me dream it into being. Also to the entire editorial and creative team that quite literally made this book, thank you for seeing the importance and value of somatic therapy during these undeniable times. Thank you for trusting this work as needed in the world.

My Rachaels, thank you for your unwavering, downright devotional support in writing this book during the hardest time of my life. Thank you for your insights, your encouragement, your mirroring, your embodied wisdom, your sharing and listening. Your direct influence in these pages is the song this book sings.

Lexi, my tried-and-true and exquisitely capable friend, thank you for your sanity, your friendship, your getting by together in school, your colleagueship, your sisterhood, and your generative ideas and modeling that infuse themselves into this book in every page. It is an honor to walk with you. You help people be more themselves.

My trusted committee, Amy Reed, Peach Friedman, Ruthie Fraser, Cailey Halloran, Alex Smith, Elizabeth Astor, and Sara Emmitt, thank you for your impeccable eyes and unwavering cheerleading support in this project and beyond. For encouraging me to write a book again and again. For believing when I didn't. For being excited when I was tired. For your mirroring. For all the ways you have reflected what is real and true, and for the ways you inspire by embodying yourselves.

Without clear and consistent mentorship I believe it is difficult to hone the art of somatic therapy. It requires receiving attendance, presence, and deep listening. It requires modeling curiosity and authenticity. I am very lucky to have been mentored well. To my clinical mentors Leah D'Abate and Arielle Schwartz, whose influence radiates like subtle moonshine across these pages and in all the work I am privileged to offer, may the long lines of health you support stream into the world always. I am forever grateful for your guidance.

I have two longtime teachers for the two practices I love the most. Their presence in my life has bestowed upon me a great gift—direct and accessible pathways home to myself. My apprenticeship to their methods, approaches, and modeling of an education that yields more of myself is a privilege to have accessed in this lifetime. One of my hopes for those who read this book is that they too can find a teacher that inspires, uplifts, and tells the truth. To my gracious and ferocious teachers, Christina Sell and Melissa Michaels, thank you for the grace of your teachings. Without your pivotal and consistent education I would be a different person, with a different life, and this book would not exist. Period.

It is a challenge as a parent to let your child have their own life filled with their own dreams, aspirations, mistakes, and hurts. My parents have faced this challenge whole-heartedly. They embody patience, tenacity, resilience, and unconditional love, having taught me about dream seeking, soul searching, and unwavering listening to what is hard. The richness of my relationship to both of my parents is one that has been carved by many of the practices, principles, and lessons in this book. And for the gift of this embodied life—for the very vehicle through which I am alive and all the particular intricacies it brings forth—I bow in deep gratitude to my unconditionally loving parents.

To Olive, who was patient, kind, and curious as her mommy did something big. Thank you for the opportunity to learn about moving and being all over again. For the plentiful kisses and squeezes and for giving me the pleasure of knowing both unencumbered presence and the terror of ferocious love. May you continue to grow while knowing and staying close enough to yourself that you feel free always.

And, to Elliot, thank you. Thank you. Thank you. Thank you. Thank you. For this wild, messy, holy, and dignified life that is forever woven between us.

About the Author

Livia Shapiro is a fresh and radically honest voice in the fields of somatic psychology and yoga. Her teaching and writing are known for their clarity, nuance, and witty humor. She is a frequent guest of podcasts on topics including somatic psychology, trauma-sensitive yoga, attachment-oriented education, and embodied spiritual practice. A longtime yoga and movement teacher, Livia has been educating and mentoring yoga teachers in somatic psychology through her learning platform Applied Psychology for Yogis since 2012. Her private somatic therapy practice facilitates women's psychological healing, embodiment, holistic development, and spiritual emergence. She graduated cum laude from the University of Vermont and holds a master's of somatic counseling psychology from Naropa University. Livia lives in Boulder, Colorado, with her family.

Printed in the USA
CPSIA information can be obtained
at www.ICGtesting.com
CBHW080808060824
12750CB00004B/10

9 781646 040957